MW00808576

LEADING FROM THE MARGINS

LEADING FROM THE MARGINS

*College Leadership
from Unexpected
Places*

MARY DANA HINTON

JOHNS HOPKINS UNIVERSITY PRESS
Baltimore

Johns Hopkins University Press
2715 North Charles Street
Baltimore, Maryland 21218
www.press.jhu.edu

Library of Congress Cataloging-in-Publication Data

Names: Hinton, Mary Dana, 1970– author.
Title: Leading from the margins : college leadership
from unexpected places / Mary Dana Hinton.
Description: Baltimore, Maryland : Johns Hopkins University Press, 2024. |
Includes bibliographical references and index.
Identifiers: LCCN 2023029964 | ISBN 9781421448510 (hardcover) |
ISBN 9781421448527 (ebook)
Subjects: LCSH: Educational leadership—United States. | Minorities in higher
education—United States—Social conditions. | Women in higher education—
United States—Social conditions. | Marginality, Social—United States.
Classification: LCC LB2805 .H54 2024 |
DDC 371.2/0110973—dc23/eng/20230805
LC record available at https://lccn.loc.gov/2023029964

A catalog record for this book is available from the British Library.

*Special discounts are available for bulk purchases of this book. For more information,
please contact Special Sales at specialsales@jh.edu.*

To the memory of my mother, Susie Ann Hinton,
and to my friend Bettie White Cooper,
both of whom have stood beside me in the margins

CONTENTS

ACKNOWLEDGMENTS

I would like to acknowledge the help and support of many who made this work possible. First, my family's humor, unyielding willingness to listen to my ramblings, and patience are directly responsible for this work. Thank you, Robert, Hallela, Hillel, and Hosanna.

My Hollins University cabinet and board of trustees are a forceful and encouraging cheering section. I'm so grateful for each of you.

Kathryn Enke, my original thought partner, was indispensable in getting this book published. Thank you for your deep care, keen eyes, and honest feedback. You make the margins better.

LEADING FROM THE MARGINS

Introduction

Those in the margins are always trying to get to the center, and those at the center, frequently in the name of tradition, are trying to keep the margins at a distance. Part of the identity of a place is the tension between those in the margins and those in the center, and they all live behind the walls which wear the tradition.

—ANNA DEAVERE SMITH, *Talk to Me*

I took on one of the most daunting challenges of my career in 2019: a TEDx talk. This opportunity required me to confront several fears at once. First, I had to agree to become a local celebrity, with marketing materials featuring my name and likeness shared across the community. Second, I had to speak in public, without the comforts of written notes, a podium, or an understudy. Third, I agreed to tell my story, a personal narrative that had previously been carefully hidden behind my professional persona. And finally, I was expected to deliver my TEDx talk from center stage, standing on a large red dot designed for a single speaker.

It was the final challenge that was most uncomfortable. Even though I was a leader in national higher education and in the local community, center stage was not my home. Ultimately, I resisted all the stage manager's cues, and I began my TEDx talk offstage, delivering the following remarks:

Look. I'm over here. I know you expect me to be at the center, but to be honest, I'm not built to be in the center. The world tells me I was made to dwell in the margins. Your inability to see me isn't a new experience for me. It's the very definition of being marginal. There are entire communities of people we fail to see because they dwell in margins. People whose humanity is doubted or, at best, questioned. People whose human value is defined by their race or gender or economic standing and, because we fail to meet a standard set by those in the center, we are left to the margins.

The margins: that place where people who are deemed unworthy are relegated. The margins: that place where you embrace who you are but feel like you're often alone. The margins: that place where you feel a visceral pain because the world tells you you're not enough and that to be enough means you would have to be a fundamentally different person. I know some of you get what I'm saying. For reasons beyond your control too, you've been relegated to the margins. Invisible. Ignored.

As someone who was born poor, Black, and a woman, the margins are *my genesis, my shelter, and my place of nourishment*. Because I come from and now choose to dwell in the margins, I have had to learn how to navigate life and leadership differently than those who come from, or primarily locate themselves in, the center.[1]

I began my talk, and now this book, with these words as a way of greeting all my fellow margin dwellers, letting them know they are not alone. You see, for those leaders who dwell in the margins, it is important to acknowledge what brought—and keeps—us there. My margins are drawn by my sex, race, and class. These factors not only draw my margins but also help me to embrace my margins and my leadership.

Perspectives formed by life in the margins give us new ways of viewing the world, a readiness to question inherited assumptions, and the tools to give witness to the harm these assumptions cause. So, as a leader from the margins, you step into this work to engage the center in these questions and to engage (and recruit) other marginalized communities who share these gifts of perspective and wisdom.

To be clear, I am not advocating for a better or worse way of leadership based on proximity to the margin. I am, however, acknowledging that one can conceive of a leadership position born from the margins. And because this leadership starts from a different point, it will, by design, manifest itself differently. It will have meaning for leaders who look different. Leaders who have defied (and continue to defy) great odds will have a different approach not easily recognized or valued by those from the center. Leadership from the margins demands a different skill set. A different path. A different destination. While one might think a leader from the margins seeks the center, I argue that a leader from the margins seeks to move across that space and reach individuals and circumstances in other margins. This book is for leaders who proudly emerge from the margins and who seek to serve and support others like themselves. This book is for leaders who find themselves captivated by the very existence of margins and what they mean. Let's travel there.

Defining Margins

Margin, like most words, is readily defined. It is "the edge or border of something" or "an amount by which a thing is won or falls short."[2] Even more, most readers know margins from their own daily experience. We can readily name the borders of a margin: top, bottom, left, right. In its most simplistic meaning, the margin is the space on a sheet of paper that provides the boundaries for contents on the page. But margins have additional meanings. For example, in investment lingo, a margin is when you utilize your broker's resources to enhance your investment power. You can get wealthier, faster, if you navigate the margins carefully. When speaking of social justice, margins refer to a dwelling place for those who have been relegated to the outside of mainstream society: the vulnerable, the different, the hurt, the displaced. There are even moments when margins are defined simply, quickly, and without nuance: you look different than me; you sound different than me; you speak a different first language than I do; you worship differently than I do. The world today emphasizes the negative aspects of difference as a means to create boundaries—or margins—that define good/bad, rich/poor, able/disabled, Black/white. How we see and navigate these differences creates new and different margins every day—some self-imposed and others imposed by society, status, or history.

When we talk about the margins in a contested civic society like contemporary America, we are talking about the people who don't matter. Those who have been denied a seat at the table or a voice in our politics. Those who, when we picture the typical American in our head, are erased. This mechanism—let's call it marginalization—isn't an accident or an unanticipated outcome of the unfolding of history. The marginalization of much of the nation's inhabitants was the product of a system that actively pushed certain segments of the population aside, into the shadows, off the stage, to the margins.

These margins where women leaders, immigrant leaders, and leaders of color dwell are not neutral spaces. Remember the second definition described above: "the amount by which a thing . . . falls short." As the value-laden corollary of *margin, marginal* reflects the valuation that others place on your background and preparation for leadership. It implies a position that is temporary and minimal, a very narrow space of existence, something close to the limit, something of little value. Women have often been viewed as marginal when it comes to leadership. If one overlays being a woman of color, particularly an African American woman, negative value gets attached to your leadership ability and desirability.

One captivating part of margins is that they enliven a dialectical, meaning they present equally valid opposing forces. Alongside the negative aspects of difference is an alternate, enriching perspective about margins waiting to emerge. For example, while margins are often thought of as extra, perhaps even dispensable, space on the page, they are also necessary. Margins provide the frame for the important content on a page—and in life. On the most important documents and decrees in history, we find margins. They provide guidance to what matters most. Margins can direct us to what is life-giving, impactful, and sustaining. We honor the language, ideas, and words within a text by framing them with a margin.

Margins are often thought of as boundaries or constraints. Yet, they could just as easily signal where we begin—a roadmap for upward or forward movement. Every human who has written has looked, apprehensively, at the margin and considered how to free the first word onto the page. The margin can intimidate us with its quiet, patient waiting. Yet the margin beckons us to write the first word, share the first thought. The margin frees us to become who we hope to be on the page.

Margins can also be an invitation to engagement or creativity. The margins, perhaps even those on the pages in this book, provide a space on which to jot one's most immediate and insightful thoughts. Margins are the supreme blank space, perhaps perceived as signaling nothing; and yet, they are where we jot our most intimate, most compelling, and most vulnerable thoughts. We reveal ourselves in the margins of books. We are our truest selves when we step outside of the center and hear only our own voice, which is what the margin beckons. It is within the margins that we discover who we truly are. The blank space enables us to reveal, and revel in, our creativity that is perhaps too foreboding to imagine sharing with the world. Perhaps your margins are for your inner artist, allowing you to make your books and journals a living museum in tribute to you. In the margins, we find safety. The margins welcome us. The margins are where our voices come alive. The margins unleash our creative selves.

Each of us must determine how we locate ourselves in the dialectic of margins. Are they constraining boundaries that merely offer limits? Are they benign borders? Or, are they places where we find ourselves, our voices, and our opportunities? How we experience the margins is largely based on our primary orientation to the margin. For those of us who dwell in the margins, they are viewed as beginnings, points of orientation, starting places, sanctuaries. For those who hail from the center, for whatever reasons, margins become boundaries, constraints, places to avoid. Margins literally and figuratively create the distinct lines and sharp edges that separate individual thoughts, classes, and access points. In either instance, how we lead is dramatically impacted by our experience of this space.

Finding Oneself in the Margins

Often when leaders are described, it seems it was inevitable that the person would become a leader from a young age. They had the opportunities, privileges, and even physical characteristics (are all leaders tall?) to be a leader. A recent study found that when asked to picture a leader, both men and women identified a leader as a man: "Getting noticed as a leader in the workplace is more difficult for women than for men. Even when a man and a woman were reading the same words off a script, only the man's leadership potential was recognized."[3] Women are not who we have traditionally pictured as leaders, and, as a result, women have less access to leadership development, training, and mentoring opportunities. Women frequently get relegated to the margins.[4]

Next, let's add race to the margin. According to the American Council of Education, only 5 percent of college presidents are women of color, with 25 percent of college presidents being white women.[5] Women lead 8 percent of Fortune 500 companies—a record number, despite women making up nearly 60 percent of the workforce in the United States.[6] Of the 41 Fortune 500 leaders who are women, 6 are women of color, and only 2 are African American women (my demographic).[7]

Taken separately, my sex and race make a leadership role less likely. Taken together, given current structures, my being a leader feels increasingly impossible. This perspective is only heightened when you consider the lack of access I have had to opportunities and resources that support leadership development. I was raised in a low-income household in the rural South, with few pathways to leadership. In fact, a 2014 study found that low-income and first-generation college students were significantly less likely to pursue campus leadership roles than their higher-income peers, even after controlling for demographic and other variables.[8] This early lack of opportunity for engagement has implications for long-term success, as the networking and leadership skills developed at the collegiate level are not always allowed to emerge for low-income students.

I am not a tall, white male who grew up with the privilege such markers can afford, though, of course, that privilege can readily vary based on individual circumstances. I am a leader who emerged from the margin. A leader who longed to hear from others like me—people who, perhaps unexpectedly, found themselves in leadership roles wondering how to navigate when one's core perspective is not centered by others.

I titled this book *Leading from the Margins* because my life, my leadership, my calling, is based on the dialectics of the margins. My spirit was born and shaped in marginal spaces. I believe leadership is about bringing those on the margins to and through the center, as well as helping those in the center explore their margins. My life on the margins supports my ability to move not only toward the center but through the center to reach and uplift others on the margins. Similarly, leadership from the margins can equip those in the center to recognize and value those on the margins.

Exploring the Margins

This book is organized with three margins. In part I, I draw the lines of the page that have most shaped my leadership and invite you to consider what has most shaped your leadership. In chapter one, you will learn my story about living in the margins. I share the early experiences that helped me to frame who I am and contribute to how I lead from the margins today. Throughout the book, I invite you to consider your own story and what shaped your starting position. What drove your marginality? Did you emerge from the margins? Do you have an affinity for or responsibility to those from the margins? From where did that responsibility emerge? In chapter two, I continue my narrative beyond my childhood in Kittrell, North Carolina, to my first leadership roles in higher education.

My narrative and my marginality are framed by three distinct aspects of my identity: my race, my gender, and my socioeconomic status as a student. In chapter three, I explore the role race plays in shaping identity. I summarize the research surrounding race and the data about how race is reflected in leadership roles and expectations of leaders. I share those moments where race played a framing role not only in how I was shaped on the margins but in how it has impacted my ability to lead from the margins. Since the shaping role of race is not merely a part of an origin story, I also explore how it continues to play a significant role in how I lead and how my leadership is perceived by others.

Chapter four turns a similarly critical eye to the role of gender and leadership, and what the data tell us about women's leadership. Gender has played a powerful role in my life and in the lives of many on the margins, so I turn to those framing events. Gender is a central identity and shapes the leadership style of people. This is likely clear for most women and for those who do not fit the gender norms of leadership. However, since leadership literature and expectations typically normalize masculinity, gender may be a less salient leadership identity to cisgender males. Please know, male readers, that this chapter is also relevant for you.

Finally, chapter five looks at the role of socioeconomic status and rurality in shaping the margins. Like race and gender, class is often a direct determining factor in one's marginality and the opportunities one has available to them. I explore this further and review the data about class mobility and how it impacts leadership.

Part II seeks to take the data and personal narratives of part I and discern what they mean for the practice of leadership. Broad leadership development theory based on the margins is framed in chapter six. What is effective leadership, regardless of orientation to the margins? What does being from the margins imply for an effective leader today? How can you leverage your leadership from the margins to enhance your leadership endeavors? Chapter seven addresses vocational obligations that emerge as one leads from the margins. How do leaders from the margins understand their vocation?

Part III explores the callings that emerge from leading from the margins. Within this section, I share some of the strategies I've employed and advice I've received to make leadership from the margins a bit easier. Chapter eight examines the specific implications of leading from the margins for those in the most senior executive roles. It navigates the adage that leadership is not about the leader and confronts head-on the fact that, often, it is all about you. The roles of gratitude and courage, both critical to leaders from the margins, are shared in chapter nine, along with a conversation about sponsorship, mentoring, and support—key expressions of gratitude. Chapter ten interrogates the demands of the margins and shares cautions from the margins that I have found valuable over time.

The concluding chapter is designed to invite you to think about the possibility of your own leadership. Your starting point. Your narrative. Your boundaries. Your influences. Your margins. I provide three; you provide the fourth. I invite you to locate yourself within this book and travel with me to the margins of leadership.

PART I

The Margins Emerge

CHAPTER 1

An Origin Story

Your margin is my opportunity.

—JEFF BEZOS

I began this book by saying my life is in the margins. This non-neutral space—this space that has so much power over what we attend to and what we ignore—has shaped not only my journey but also my approach to that journey, and it has fashioned a call to help others. It also shapes how I choose to lead those who are entrusted to me. To dwell within the margins forces a person to develop, nurture, and rely upon characteristics that enable that person to not just survive but to thrive. While thriving may not feel possible when growing up or early on in one's career, the characteristics developed in the margin can yield essential leadership qualities.

For many emerging leaders, a common question is, How much should my personal experiences and background inform my leadership? I wrestled with this question a great deal and frequently found myself asking leaders I deeply respect, often from the margins themselves, for their advice: "Did you allow your background to influence your leadership?" Nearly without exception, each of these leaders responded, "Yes!" Their background from the margins—which varied dramatically—had helped to frame their leadership and became an asset. They, too, admitted that they had wrestled with this early in their careers. Why? Because few leadership books mention the strengths, skills, values, habits, and ideals developed on the margins. To the contrary, poverty, race or experience with racism, being a woman, being a first-generation American or a first-generation college student, and other margin-bound characteristics are often described as factors to overcome, as implied deficits, rather than a source of leadership strength. Therefore, when one recognizes that these factors are shaping leadership priorities and strategies, one begins to question whether their influence is appropriate or valuable.

This questioning intensifies when you recognize that even if you attempt to hide those characteristics, others will actively seek out your perspective and insights about those topics. While there is great wisdom in striving not to be defined by a single characteristic or identity, the reality is that the world has its own perception of you and people will seek you out because of their perspective on those characteristics and identities. For example, while I may, at times, mightily resist being labeled "a woman president" or "a Black president," I cannot ignore those key parts of my identity, as those are often important signifiers for myself and those I lead in my role as a college president. In higher education, students who sense a resonance or see a leader who "looks like them" are often hungry to talk with someone who understands their perspective. Those parts of ourselves that leadership books may encourage us to hide, resist, or overcome have the power to make us attractive to the people we are leading. More about that later.

In this chapter, I begin to share my personal journey and how it has helped build my leadership perspective. The chapter continues with an exploration of how one's life on the margin uniquely prepares and equips one to lead toward, and through, the center and provides the skills needed to help the leadership of others from the margins emerge. You will have an opportunity to think through how your personal journey and background in and around the margins can empower your leadership.

Margin Demography

My own experience in the margins is based on my race, gender, and socioeconomic class. My identity, my authentic voice, was nurtured in rural North Carolina. My origin story, comprised of poverty and too many racist experiences to count, is not a story that one shares when attending a New England liberal arts college or when leading in predominately white institutions. My "delightful" and "quaint" Southern accent only served to mark me as other. So, my voice and my story, and things that could help a person discern my story, were silenced and quietly packed away because they marked me as vulnerable. As weak. As not a leader. As in the margins.

As a Black woman who grew up in poverty in the rural South, I can see that there are many dimensions that inform and support my leadership. I say this recognizing that people from the center might suggest these factors undermine my leadership. Therefore, to truly understand how those factors both influence and support leadership, I have had to consciously look at my own journey in the margins. For me, that intentional self-understanding began by closely examining my origin story.

Raj Chetty, a Harvard economist, developed the Opportunity Atlas in 2018 to provide data needed to explore the role of childhood neighborhood demographics in future outcomes. By matching childhood census data with how much people earn in their thirties, the data "provide information on the average *actual* outcomes of children who grew up in each area. Each estimate is specific to a selected group of children from each tract, defined by their race, gender, and parental income level. For instance, one estimate might look at the outcomes in adulthood for black men who grew up in low-income families in a specific tract."[1]

The website goes on to note, "Traditional measures of poverty and neighborhood conditions provide snapshots of income and other variables for residents in an area at a given point in time." In contrast, Opportunity Atlas uses detailed longitudinal data, following individuals from their neighborhood of birth to their outcomes many years later "to study how economic *opportunity* varies across neighborhoods. . . . Using the Atlas, you can see not just where the rich and poor currently live—which was possible in previously available data from the Census Bureau—but whether children in a given area tend to grow up to become rich or poor."[2] Outcomes included within the Opportunity Atlas include income at age 35, incarceration rates, teenage pregnancy rates, high school and college graduation rates, number of children, and percentage remaining in the same neighborhood where they grew up. Regional differences are stark, with rural areas across the South showing the least mobility out of poverty across these multiple measures.

While I predate the current Opportunity Atlas data by eight years (I was born in 1970 and the Opportunity Atlas begins with those born in 1978), there is no reason for me to assume that the data do not reasonably mirror my own experience. I spent the preponderance of my childhood, from grades three to ten, in US Census tract 37181961000, Kittrell, North Carolina. For all children in my approximate cohort between 2012 and 2016, the average household income at age 35 was $34,000, with an average individual income of $24,000. The teen birthrate for women in the cohort overall was 33 percent. The poverty rate for the tract between 2012 and 2016 was 28 percent. Nearly half (49 percent) were single parents during that same time frame. Overall, 38 percent of my tract cohort were married at age 35 and the employment rate was 75 percent at the same age. A little over 60 percent of the group remained in the commuting zone as adults.

The picture changes significantly when I overlap the race, gender, and household income demographic factors that best match my own identities. When I select for Black, female, and low-income women—my own descriptors growing up—the outcomes shift. The average household income at age 35 drops to $25,000, a 27 percent decrease. A 13 percent decrease is seen for individual income, which drops to $21,000. The employment rate increases to 80 percent (meaning Black women work slightly more than women overall), despite the lower earnings. The teen birthrate, 33 percent for the overall group, is greater than 50 percent for my cohort.

To explore this data is to see that the cards are stacked against the residents in this community. And yet this community produced leaders, I among them. Please allow me to be clear: I do not ascribe to the "pull yourself up by your bootstraps" mentality. This notion that one can do anything with the appropriate will is demoralizing and dishonest for those with plenty of will but no way to achieve their goals. While success does require a host of skills to make the best of every situation, the reality is that good fortune, lucky breaks, fortuitous support, and perhaps some divine intervention also play a large role. There are deeply entrenched political, economic, and social systems that create opportunity; and systems that, no matter how hard you try personally, are structured to make demographics your destiny. I am very proud of the work I have done, but I've made educational equity my life's mission because I am keenly aware that I was lucky. I do not want entrenched racist, sexist, and classist systems to continue to prevent young people from achieving success.

Defiance within the Margins

This desire to exact change and not allow inequitable systems to determine the course of one's life has helped me to develop a strong sense of mission and is the foundation of my leadership. Yet to embrace leadership in the face of one's unfavorable demographic odds often results in the need to be defiant.

As such, within the margins, much of my life has been defined by defiance. Anyone who knows me will find this statement somewhat perplexing. By all appearances, I am likely the least defiant person you'll meet. I wear pink shoes unironically. I believe in the inherent goodness in all people, even challenging people who have repeatedly proven themselves unworthy of my belief in them. I feel poorly when people laugh at one another, and I tend to avoid conflict. I'm a people pleaser at heart. My family teases me and calls me Pollyanna. My leadership cabinet jokes about my not using profanity and (sometimes) feels bad using it in my presence. I'm more likely to cry than yell, though both are quite rare. I sometimes publicly mock myself, pretending to pound on tables to get my point across. In this situation, others usually laugh along with (at?) me because it's unimaginable that I would react so vehemently.

Yet, for much of my life, I've been vehemently defying the world. While no credit is due to me for the first defiant action—being born to an impoverished 45-year-old in 1970 when "geriatric births" were much less common—my defiant nature has, I suppose, been around since my arrival. But that entrance aside, my defiance has been textbook and intentional: a visceral, bold resistance against an opposing force or authority.

Here's my earliest remembered example of my defiant nature emerging. Picture it: It's the mid-1980s in rural North Carolina. I'm likely wearing a Jheri curl, thrilled that my mother had the money to pay for me to get one. She had to work for days to afford such a luxury. Why would she be willing to do that? Well, we all buy luxury sometimes. For some, it's a nice car or home or vacation. For others, it's the luxury of not having to stand over a hot stove in North Carolina in the summer, doing your child's hair. It's helping her hair grow so that she's not mocked by white kids for being a "pickaninny" or by Black kids for having hair like a "rat's nest," both jabs I became intimately familiar with while growing up pre–Jheri curl. Sometimes you can't win.

While I cannot recall my exact hairstyle at the time, I do clearly remember being in junior high school completing a career assessment—you know, the kind you do in middle school homeroom. *What do you like to do? What do you dislike? What are your strengths? What are your weaknesses?* You get the drift.

At that point in my life, standardized anything was a relative strong suit for me. This is not because I was smart (the GRE, ACT, and SAT all illustrated my deficits, at least according to the ambiguous standards that fuel them), but rather because I was a good reader and could focus on details. For the California Achievement Test and similar standardized tests of that time, that's all you needed. And, everyone—including those who called me "pickaninny" and "rat's nest"—knew I was good at standardized tests. (This was pre-FERPA, when academic performance was discussed as openly and joyfully as the day's lunch menu.)[3] I dominated the bubble sheet and looked forward to this assignment. Would I be lauded for my career assessment prowess? Would others finally realize that I was more than a hairstyle and crossed eyes?

So, I get my booklet encased in a sealed envelope, bubble sheet, and No. 2 pencil. I prepare to excel. I tear open the envelope, and with a sniff of the new booklet, I prepare to fill out the early questions. Name, address, phone number. And then, the most challenging question I'd encountered to that point in my academic career: What are your parents' titles: Mr. and Mrs.; Mr.; Mrs.; Miss (there was implied disapproval next to that one, I seem to recall); or Dr. and Mrs.?

Now let me be clear: at this point in my life in rural North Carolina, I'd probably never heard the word *feminist*. I was patently unaware of the movement and of the complications of the movement for women of color. I was unaware of intersectionality. I had no idea about womanists; first-, second-, or third-wave feminists; or Audre Lorde or Betty Friedan. I just knew something was fundamentally wrong with that list in the booklet, as it completely left off the option of Dr. and Mr.

I'm not sure why I fixated on this omission at that time. My response to the question should have been easy: fill in the bubble that said "Mrs." I was being raised by a single mother, as my father had died when I was 10. I also knew to fill in "Mrs." because for decades after my father's death, my mother still asked to be listed as Mrs. Robert Hinton in the phone book. My mother was a complicated, independent woman, and I never understood her request, but it did make this career assessment question an easy one: fill in "Mrs."!

Yet, I remember staring at the booklet, obsessing over why there wasn't an option for Dr. and Mr. Was that title impossible? Why couldn't that happen? Who got to decide? I spent nearly the entire testing time thinking about the issue and what I was going to do about it. Should I tell someone? Who? Who would care? Who would even understand why this felt so wrong? Did I even understand? (Suffice to say, my career assessment results were less than stellar.) I decided in that moment that I would try to one day be Dr. and Mr. I didn't know how or why. I didn't know when. I had no plan in mind. But I swore I would not let this go unaddressed. I had to get a Dr. of some sort so I could show them.

I recall lying awake at night wondering how I could make Dr. and Mr. happen. Would no man want a woman Dr. if he weren't a Dr.? Was I willing to risk my romantic future to defy a bubble sheet that mattered little? In the end, I realized it wasn't about the form or about getting married, it was about defiance and marginality and not discounting my future before I even had a chance to think about it. It was about what was right. And just. And equitable. I know now that I was having a painful visceral reaction to injustice, to being on the margins. I planned my gender role defiance in seventh grade. It was then, in a classroom in rural North Carolina, that my feminist-womanist defiance was consciously born.

My defiant soul hasn't looked back since.

More powerfully than it probably should have, this early moment of defiance began the process of defining my self-understanding as a woman and my earliest attempts to embrace my life on the margins and proclaim its value. Though I was unaware of it at the time, it was the moment when I experienced that not only are the expectations for women different, but we are defined largely in comparison to men. The margins were defined in comparison to the center. The notion that a woman could attain the highest levels of education and still choose to marry was a foreign one according to a "standardized" test. My determination then was to get as much education as possible to defy expectations. Today, I am a part of a Dr. and Mr. couple, but we don't have the same last name, so the title piece is irrelevant. What is relevant is that I learned in seventh grade that as a woman I would be asked to define myself against what society expected of me—that, as someone from the margins, I was being consciously taught to define myself in relation to the center. This first, perhaps small but formative, recognition of my marginality was closely followed by another one of much greater consequence.

As I will discuss later in greater detail, growing up Black in the rural South in the 1970s and '80s was a challenging experience: we lived critical race theory, we didn't theorize about it. Very few people of my generation could afford to be defiant racially. If we attempted to go against the standards set by the majority, we were asked, "Who do you think you are?" or told, "Get back in your place!" Or, worse yet, words took a backseat to violence as defiance was punished through physical harm or even death threats and forced submission to racist systems. If one rankled the racial norms within the Black community, we were called

"Uncle Tom" or "Oreo"—Black on the outside, white on the inside. While my white friends were navigating the traditional perils of adolescence—boys, cliques, smoking—I was trying to navigate identity politics without any exposure to or understanding of the term and without any insight into how to navigate them. My goal was not merely to fit in. It was to understand how to construct a space wherein I could dwell as just myself. Wherein I could be me and that was seen as sufficient.

In tenth grade, I had the courage to ask my guidance counselor to help me think about college, as this appeared to be the way forward.

Even now, more than 30 years later, I can picture this tableau. We were in her office as I excitedly explained how my sister was at Dartmouth College. (Okay, so I was probably bragging. My sister had participated in the A Better Chance (ABC) program, but I had not been accepted into the program.) I asked what I needed to do to get to college. I recall I was taller than this woman and that she had to look up to make eye contact. Eye contact is important when eviscerating someone, particularly if you want to make certain that you eliminate all hopes and dreams in the process.

In her elderly, Southern drawl, she explained that college was not an option for me, as a Black woman. I give the woman credit for introducing intersectionality in my life (race + gender = an increased negative impact of both). She told me no. She told me, essentially, that my place in the world (on the margins) had been defined by others and that I was to simply accept that place. To not even dream of something more. In her mind, her job wasn't to help me define my success or pursue that success. Her goal was to ensure that my success was small, my hopes even smaller, and my opportunities limited. Her goal was to conceal equity from me, to make certain that I didn't think, much less expect, that I could move beyond my current circumstance. Her goal was to reduce me in the margins and remind me of my marginality.

And, for a longer time than I care to admit, she was successful. For too long, I questioned my ability because of my demographics. I internalized some portion of what she said and doubted myself. I read the encounter as a failure on my part when, in reality, the failure was hers. With the most generous assessment, she simply failed to imagine a Black woman succeeding in the world. And yet, I chose, even as she spewed her vitriol, to be defiant. At that moment, I knew I would go to college. I didn't know how or where. But her telling me no was the most motivating thing she could have said; defiance propelled me forward.

I have often been asked why, in that moment, I made the decision to be defiant by embracing the margins. To be honest, it was a survival strategy. I was defiant because I did not want to spend my life in poverty. I was defiant because I could not see a way out of my current circumstance other than education. Who was this woman, who didn't even know me, to decide what my future would be? I became defiant because I had nothing else to lose. For me, defiance was a positive motivating force and a strength I gained from living on the margins. I hasten to add that I completely understand and feel great empathy for the many young people who find themselves in a similar moment and choose to defy in less productive ways.

My defiance at that moment also meant that I had to go home and defy a few more norms, yet another task many young people face today. It was rare that I would go home and share my day with my mother. She had other things going on, and the adolescent happenings in my high school were likely of limited interest, not because she didn't care but because she was keeping us afloat. My mother was working hard to support us. She had one child at an Ivy League school, another flouncing around with curly hair and parachute miniskirts; and she worked all day cleaning Mr. and Mrs. Cooper's house. My mother had told me what to do: get an education and use that education to serve those less fortunate. She didn't need to explain much more nor did she want to hear the details about my "process." She was trying to make it in the world.

But the afternoon of this occurrence was different. My mother had told me that the only way "out" was through an education, and this counselor had told me I couldn't take that path. I knew I still needed to get out. I knew I needed to obey my mother. But I also knew this was bigger than me and that I needed help.

My mother taught me many lessons, two chief among them: (1) always work hard at whatever you do—there are no shortcuts if something is done well—and (2) do things for yourself—don't ask, and for darn sure do not expect, others to help you out.

When I went to my mother that afternoon, I imagined her advice would entail words of wisdom to figure this out and some difficult questions about why I would have even asked this woman for help. But I told her, nonetheless. And it was my mother's decision the following day to ask for and accept help from the Coopers that fundamentally changed my life. I know it wasn't easy for her to tell them we needed help. I don't know how she navigated the conversation or how she found the strength to go against all she held dear to make it happen. But I do know this: on that day she taught me that no matter how much it hurts, sometimes you must ask for help. At that moment, help came in the form of the Cooper family paying for me to go to an all-girls boarding school, which in turn led to many great things unfolding in my life.

The Coopers

Without equivocation, the second most influential people in my life—behind my mother—were Betty and Marshall Cooper. The Coopers, who were prominent in the textile industry, entered our lives in 1976 when my mother became their housekeeper. There is nothing unusual about that circumstance, as many families of means had housekeepers who not only cleaned their home, as my mother did, but also cared for the children, cooked, and were a family confidant. Despite the movie tropes, this is not some Southern romanticized notion of what "the maid" did. This was the reality of my mother's and my life.

I think it is fair to say that we and the Coopers viewed each other as family. I can say with full confidence that I saw them as people who cared deeply about me and my family. I can say, with nearly equal confidence, that my mother and Mrs. Cooper had a close and nurturing relationship. I have never heard anyone in either family say a bad thing about the other.

What made the Coopers so special to me was that they invited me into their world, a world very different from my own, while also helping me embrace my own world; and they frequently stepped into the margins alongside me. For example, when Cabbage Patch Dolls first hit the market in 1982, I, like many other kids, desperately wanted one. They were not only hard to find but—for my family—out of range financially. It was Betty Cooper who bought me a Cabbage Patch Doll. This may seem like an easy step to take, but there's more. It was Betty Cooper who argued with a salesclerk to sell her a Black Cabbage Patch Doll. It was Betty Cooper who didn't stop until I got said doll (named Barbara Brenna), despite the ridicule she experienced making such a purchase. Why does this matter? Because in 1982, Mrs. Cooper knew that representation mattered. It was not something that was widely (if at all) discussed, but she knew, and she honored me with that purchase.

It was Mr. Cooper who, when my handwriting presented me with ongoing problems in school, bought me an electric typewriter so I would not have to struggle so much. He told my mother that he hoped I was not disappointed it wasn't a computer and wondered if he should get me one of those instead. I was proud of being able to type my papers and homework and, though that did nothing to endear me to my peers, it did make my life easier. He invested, unasked, in my success.

It was also Mr. Cooper who, during a trip with their family and my mother to the beach, helped me navigate my overwhelming (and ongoing) fear of sand crabs. The Coopers would occasionally ask my mother to work for them during their summer vacations at the beach, and I was invited to go along. I loved, then and now, being on the beach and observing the ocean, but my fear of beach wildlife was real. Mr. Cooper would fend off the sand crabs and let me know when it was safe to be outside. He reached hero status in my mind in those days.

From only these three instances, I knew that the Coopers cared about me as a person. They wanted to make sure I had what I needed to be successful, and they believed in my potential. Even when I couldn't see my potential, they saw it and surrounded me with the support I needed to thrive. The Coopers were among the kindest people I had ever met.

By today's standards, perhaps these stories seem trite or unmeaningful. To me, they changed my life. Through actions and example, the Coopers told me I was worthy. And when my public high school guidance counselor shared that Black women don't go to college, the Coopers literally and without equivocation changed my life.

My mother and the Coopers went to great lengths to get me out of a school that did not support my aspirations or my potential, and that was a transformative moment in my life. Without hesitation, the Coopers worked to get me into and paid for my attendance at Saint Mary's School in Raleigh, North Carolina, which was Mrs. Cooper's alma mater.

I still regularly thank Mrs. Cooper for their help. Sadly, Mr. Cooper died in 2017. To this day, Mrs. Cooper demurs and says they really didn't do anything, that I did all the hard work. She credits my success to my resilience and effort. I credit it to my family, the support of the Coopers, and a commitment to my mission to make sure other young women don't have to rely on a lucky break or a single kind family to be successful.

Had that series of events not happened—had a vitriolic, simple-minded, racist woman not uttered those words in the counselor's office and the Coopers not immediately stepped up—I don't know whether I would be where I am today. The world that the counselor embodied in her response to me had set limited expectations for people who are impoverished, for women, and for people of color—for all of us on the margins. Expectations that required a fundamental shift in action to thwart. Because I was given the opportunity of an education and because people, starting with my mother and the Coopers, sacrificed for me to have those opportunities, I had to work that much harder.

My mother taught me that a legacy of grit and resilience does not come neatly wrapped and tied with a bow. She taught me that I should look at students and see that the rough edge they have that may be off-putting to some, an edge she and I share, is simply that young person trying their best to not only survive but thrive. The grit and resilience my mother bequeathed to me could only have been gifted on the margins. (Not incidentally, this grit has led to no small part of my fundraising success as a college president. If my mother could risk it all for me, then surely I can take a risk by inviting people to cocreate a young person's future through a financial gift.)

These moments of defiance in the margins ultimately served me well. I had to work consciously, explicitly, and diligently to be defiant and successful. I often conjure up these moments to motivate me on dark, tired, and weary days. I recall my mother's swollen knees when she returned home from scrubbing floors all day, and I remind myself that the same spirit that defied those odds of getting out of poverty reside within me. I chose, and choose, defiance. The margins remain a source of strength.

My defiance didn't end with setting goals for myself regarding gender and race. It was defiance that enabled me to persevere as one of only two or three women of color at Saint Mary's School, and as questions about my hair grew tiring and I was never invited on weekend trips. (I couldn't have afforded to go, but an invitation would have been nice.) It was active defiance that enabled me to stand up to people who suggested or said outright that I was only at Williams College due to affirmative action. (I'm looking at you, legacy jock admit.) It was defiance that enabled me to survive when I had no financial safety net after college and for most of my adulthood. It was defiance to decide I could get my PhD while pregnant and working full-time, to become the Dr. of Dr. and Mr.

It was defiance that planted the first seed of becoming a leader in academia. When a "colleague" said at a conference that students of color bring a culture of oppression with them to campus that ensures they can't succeed, I decided that I would work on educational equity to prove to him (and the world) that it is not the students who determine their failures, it is our institutions. I get angry just remembering someone suggesting that students from the margins want to fail and are intrinsically designed to do so. It is defiance that enables me to speak my truth to those presidential colleagues who want to dismiss the role of education in creating social equity (and inequity). These are leaders who, because of the privilege to which they have become accustomed, cannot even recognize that their most important work isn't perpetuating the status quo, it's breaking it apart and facilitating the development and rights of all. It is an act of defiance when I wear my pink shoes, when I hug my students, and when I make myself vulnerable. Leaders don't do those things, I am told. *Yes, they do*, I say defiantly, and I work even harder toward success to prove them wrong and to find kindred spirits in the margins.

There are as many ways to lead and be successful as there are people. One doesn't have to look a particular way to become a leader. One doesn't have to use ridiculous academic jargon, play academic politics, or facilitate exclusion to be a leader in higher education. I stand in defiance of all of that. I want you to, as well.

What the Margins Frame

As you reflect on your story and background, I am sure you can recall your own examples of how the margins impacted your leadership. Being subject to the constant discounting of one's value can help to build a distinct resolve and sense of perseverance that can serve one well. Likewise, spending time intentionally on understanding your origin story can provide signals about the strengths you have been developing throughout your life: strengths that can serve you well as a leader; strengths that can also serve those you lead.

Marginality also means that your leadership will not look like the leadership of others. It will have a uniqueness that serves to make you stand out. Your experiences—and your willingness to share those experiences—signals to others that you are willing to journey with them in addition to leading them. This willingness to meet people where they are and travel with them is distinguishing and empowering to a community. Because you have traversed the margins, this is something that may come quite naturally for you to deploy.

Finally, what many leadership theories claim as a limiting factor—defiance—becomes an asset for those who hail from the margins. Being defiant for the common good provides you with the energy and insight to face great challenges and remain undeterred. At a moment when leadership is more complex and challenging than ever, I believe that leaders from the margins have an advantage in leadership.

Questions for Reflection

As you ponder how the margins can frame and support your leadership, a few questions for discernment emerge:

- Do you see elements in your background or origin story that suggest you, too, may hail from the margins?
- Can you go back to your experiences in the margins and let them sustain you when you are faced with challenges today?
- In what ways can your marginality amplify your leadership?

CHAPTER 2

Finding My Life's Work

It was my mother's work with the Coopers that was my introduction to what the Benedictines call the dignity of all work. According to the Benedictine Institute at Saint John's University:

> Dignity of Work, as referenced in chapter 48 of the *Rule of Saint Benedict*, is to "live by the labor of [one's] hands." All work, whether physical or mental, should be considered equal so the worker can appreciate the dignity of work in God's creation. We all have gifts to share with the world and Benedict saw that everyone's contribution had value and dignity to the whole.[1]

My mother took such tremendous pride in her work. She always told me, no matter my job or title, to do the work with excellence. The quote I heard often was, "You can do anything

The "What the Margins Frame" section in this chapter is adapted from Mary Hinton, "Higher Education Must Meet the Needs of an Ever-Growing Diverse Student Population." *Register Citizen*, November 4, 2010. https://www.register citizen.com/news/article/DR-MARY-HINTON-Higher-education-must-meet-the -12104693.php. Used with permission.

you want. But do it well. If you're a garbage collector, be the best garbage collector there is." Like any child growing up, I grew weary of these lectures. However, when I think about my approach to life and leadership today, it's clear those lessons took.

Working hard and trying to be the "best" is not because of my title but because it speaks to who I am as a human being. I make many mistakes, but I try to learn from them. I get tired, but I try to remember the exhaustion my mother felt after a day's work—exhaustion from doing her very best in the job she had. I am proud to have inherited her work ethic.

My Mother's Reality

In so many ways, my mother seemed almost superhuman. Her ability to plan a holiday meal months in advance and the way she could make you wither under her gaze if you made a poor outfit choice was the stuff of legends. My mother was an amazing, funny, confident woman without whom I cannot imagine my life. But, perhaps to best understand her, you have to stand in the space between the reality of her life and the way she rose above that reality in the way she lived.

According to the CDC, the reality is that a Black woman born in the 1920s had a life expectancy of less than 50 years. My mother nearly doubled her life expectancy. In a world that only wanted her to have five decades of life, her sheer and utter will to live shone forth and enabled her to rise above, living not only a long but a vibrant life. My mom's ability to simply live and breathe for 94 years signals her strength and helps you to begin to understand who she was in the face of reality.

The reality is that the world expected so little from my mother that she never even had a birth certificate. Given the time and place where she was born, the world said her life was not worthy of being officially recorded. The document that proves to the world we exist as humans was denied to her, and yet, she grew to become one of the most humane people to ever live. In fact, more than one person has told me about the ways she held them close in their darkest moments and how she helped their light shine at a time when the world was dark. My mother had this uncanny ability to let you glimpse her humanity in such a way that it made you able to embrace your own. She allowed me to be human and feel reassured because she was near. My mother was a woman whose life began without acknowledgment, and yet she spent so much of her life acknowledging the value and humanity of others and helping them to rise.

The reality is my mother lived much of her life in a world wherein systems and people wanted to tell her what she could not do. The world sought to constrain who she was and what she could become. She was born into a world that expected her to bow down and be ashamed. But Susie Hinton never played small and never wanted those around her to play small either. She rose and stood for excellence. She wanted and insisted on something more for those she loved. Her loyalty was without boundaries. This resolve is especially impressive as she was strong in a world that wanted her to doubt herself, something she steadfastly refused to do. Now, I will confess that there were moments when her strength, her courage, and her unbridled ambition for those she loved were high standards for others to rise to. But she set that standard because she wanted her family to walk with pride. To do more, have more, and be more than the reality of the world would allow.

Born into a world that sought to limit her, my mother endeavored to spend her life creating opportunities for others. She did this through her words and deeds, as well as insisting on the value of education. In fact, I remember in seventh grade when I was a little slow turning in my homework, she lectured me for hours on the meaning of the United Negro College Fund slogan at the time: "A mind is a terrible thing to waste." I have never again turned in a late assignment.

Her passion for education, a passion she passed along to every one of her children, is even more incredible because the reality is she was never granted access to the education she deserved and only attended school through the eighth grade. And yet she was, without equivocation, one of the smartest people I know. Indeed, I pity the person who thought they could talk down to or intimidate my mother. An attempt to dismiss her only reinforced her strength.

The courage and resolve that enabled her to persevere in the most difficult circumstances life had to offer often shielded a softer side. A side that came through when she made you your favorite cake when you came home. The soft side that wanted to make sure you knew you held unfettered potential when she told you could be anything. The soft side that enabled her to remember, by name, every person she encountered. In a world that so frequently handed her hate, Susie Hinton tried, in every way she knew and could, to rise up and hand out love.

I am—and you are—the beneficiary of my mother's legacy. As leaders from the margins, we, too, must rise above the reality of our circumstances. We must be determined in the face of a world that may try to break us. We must endeavor to respond to hate with love; be courageous when the world invites fear; seek to educate ourselves and support the education of those around us; and not be defined by what can be a harsh reality. We must rise and define ourselves by our own terms.

It's likely clear by now that my mother is a costar in the story of my life. The lessons I learned from her provide the foundation for my way of being in the world. In many ways, my mother was a rebel as a person and as a parent. I come by my defiant nature honestly. And, at the same time, for her, that defiance needed to be in service to something larger than myself.

For example, my mother all but forbade us to sing the national anthem, say the Pledge of Allegiance, or salute the flag. Having been born in North Carolina in 1926, my mother lived a significant portion of her life in a segregated Jim Crow South. She felt, daily, that the dream of America had not only been refused to her but used against her. We were encouraged to not honor a flag and a nation that had shown no honor to us. To this day, I feel like I am betraying her memory by singing the national anthem—a song I love.

How do I reconcile this? I believe that if I and other educators do our jobs well, we can make the hope of democracy—which I don't believe is limited to the United States—a reality. I also believe that there are few places in the world outside of the United States where, in one generation, you can find the type of economic and social mobility my mother and I reflect. I believe that the life my mother fashioned for me has allowed my hope to equal my defiance.

The Road to Saint Mary's School

In 1986, I left my mother's home and my public school and headed to Saint Mary's School, a boarding high school in Raleigh, North Carolina. I found myself 50 miles from home and, at times, the only African American woman at my high school. Later, another couple of young women joined me, but the experience was always lonely. It was challenging. I lived in a quad, and all three of my roommates were fascinated by my hair. They asked wildly inappropriate questions and made grossly inappropriate comments. I recall one roommate—who probably wondered how she got stuck with me—explaining that the only Black person she knew was her maid. This was said not to insult but to explain.

Each of these roommates became a friend during my time at Saint Mary's. It was probably during these years that I had to start deciding how I would interpret what people say to me. For me (and I am not necessarily advising this for anyone else), I learned to assume the best possible motives when people engage me. Yes, I know that people don't always have the best possible motives; but it's how I was able to, and am still able to, sleep at night. I learned how to survive in a land where I was not only different but also where difference was inherently assumed to be a bad thing. It was challenging, but it was also my opportunity. At that point in my life as a young adult, a small seed was planted, one that has only recently sprouted.

I have, for much of my life, been different. It took perhaps too long for me to not only be comfortable with that but also to embrace it. Early in my first presidency, I went to a meeting and the people with whom I was talking simply stared at me. At first, I thought it was my shoes, that they were too distracting. Then I realized that I am different in so many ways that what I had on my feet probably could not have mattered less. I was the only person of color in the room, and I had no connections to the area outside of my professional position—two significant outliers on their own—not to mention that I was in attendance to speak about change, yet another challenge. I had to remind myself to embrace my difference.

To be fair, Saint Mary's School also taught me a great deal about leadership and the critical importance of women's education. While I had my share of struggles, I learned to never view another woman as my competitor. I learned that a victory for one woman is a victory for all women. And at St. Mary's, I was encouraged in my aspirations to attend college. For that, I will be forever grateful.

Going to College

After graduating from high school, I headed off to a New England liberal arts college called Williams College. My decision to attend Williams College was driven by two things—things that I think matter to this day. First, the kindness of the admissions officer who came to Saint Mary's will never be forgotten. She spoke to me as if I had value and my future was worth something. Without a doubt, her ability and willingness to see and support me made a tremendous difference. Second, I was drawn to Williams because they took the time to have me visit campus. Campus tours were not as ubiquitous in the 1980s as they are now for many. There was no way that I could have afforded to visit on my own, but the college paid for my visit and had other students, primarily students of color and first-generation students, visit that same weekend so that I could see myself, and they themselves, at Williams. The opportunity to see oneself at an institution—representation—has always mattered, and I am delighted that there is an intentionality to that today. However, it's important to consistently reflect and support representation, even after the admissions process.

It was an honor to attend Williams College, which is consistently ranked among the top liberal arts schools in the nation.

However, as a classmate said at commencement, I feel like I should have been granted a BA, an MA, and a PhD because I had to educate so many people during my time there. The challenge of New England liberal arts colleges in the late eighties and early nineties is that they were only beginning to find their way with first-generation students, low-income students, and students of color. Centuries-old institutions like Williams had not been built for, nor their success predicated on, people like me. I won't bore you with the details, but there was more than one racially related incident on campus during my time, and there continue to be challenges.

To be clear, I am a proud Williams alum, and the school is the reason why I am so passionate about the liberal arts. In fact, my commitment to the liberal arts, especially for first-generation and low-income students and students of color, was born and nurtured in Williamstown. A liberal arts education can allow you to change the course of not only your life but the lives of countless others. Williams did that for me.

Before I arrived at Williams, I was pretty sure that I wanted to major in art history. I previously had the good fortune of taking art history at Saint Mary's and loved gazing at art. Williams' art history program is among the best in the world, so it seemed like a perfect fit. But the summer before college, I had a memorable interaction.

I was in New York City staying with my mother's cousin, Betty, and working. Betty had attended Shaw University and was a librarian on Governor's Island (then a Coast Guard installation) in New York. I spent many summers with Betty, traveling with her to the library to "help," but I mostly loved being surrounded by books. (I would be remiss if I did not mention that I also spent many NYC summers with my cousin Judy, a travel agent at that time, who supplied me with my first non-babysitting job as an assistant in a corporate travel agency. I spent a lot of time straightening brochures and dropping off plane tickets to companies. I have been working since I was 12 years old. If you count babysitting, you can back that up to 10.)

Betty was, without a doubt, our family expert on education. Whenever we had any questions about education, we went directly to her. She had "made it," and she was always willing to help others.

I clearly recall sitting with Betty and enthusiastically sharing my desire to major in art history. Betty was a gentle but formidable soul, and she listened carefully. She then explained to me that I was not going to major in art history because there were no jobs attached to that. She was very clear that I didn't have the privilege nor the luxury of "those others" at Williams to study some fancy major. Because she was Betty, I listened and decided not to major in art history.

I share that story because it took me a long time to learn that though Betty cared deeply, she was wrong (and so was then president Obama in 2014 when he said the same, though he did later apologize).[2] I would have gotten a job with an art history major. I did have the right to "live the life of the mind," to study what I wanted. But like so many first-generation college students, I received well-intentioned advice that had the potential to narrow my educational experience—to narrow my life. Low-income and first-generation students and students of color have the right to study what they'd like. This doesn't mean they don't also have the obligation or responsibility to get a job immediately upon graduation to support their families and to live. However, all too often I hear about students not being allowed to take full advantage of a liberal arts education because of this tension.

And I think it can work against students in another powerful way. For a while, before college, I thought about being a teacher. And, once again—though for different reasons—I was told that wasn't an option. In this case, the barrier was that I would not make enough money to support my family. I was told that being a teacher, while noble, was not going to yield the economic mobility we needed. I think this message is also alive and well today, as the number of students going into education is seeing a decline. This makes me sad because the very people young kids need to see are deterred from choosing the profession.

In any case, my time at Williams led to a deep love for the liberal arts. That time is also when I began to understand that the liberal arts prepare you for any and every job—even if you are an art history major.

Graduate School

Earlier, I noted how much I had to teach others at Williams College. The truth is that this wasn't just a phenomenon at a New England liberal arts college. In graduate school, that feeling perpetuated with my classmates, my teachers, and my advisors. As a young master's student, I had a particularly difficult relationship with an advisor, one that I cataloged in the following letter to him:

Hopefully this sounds familiar. It's from a conversation we had on Monday.

Me: How are you doing?
Advisor: I'm fine. How's your life?
Me: Excellent. It's busy, but that's good.

Advisor: No one makes you do all of this stuff. You do it to yourself.

This is how the conversation should have continued.

Me: No, actually my skin color makes me do it.

Advisor: What are you talking about, your skin color makes you do it? That's a bunch of malarkey.

Me: You know, this may be difficult for you to understand, what with you being a white man and all, but I learned at a very early age, as do most other Black people, that giving it your all is simply not enough. You see, someone does make me do this. It is not one particular person, but rather there are thousands, maybe millions, of people out there who, if given even the slightest chance, would tell me that doing 100 percent is not enough.

Advisor: Well, all of my graduate students give more than 100 percent. That's what separates PhD students from others. It's not a race issue.

Me: I wish you were right. But in order to even get here, I had to give many times more than what your white students gave. And even then, some people have the nerve to say I don't deserve it, that I had "an edge." What they really mean is that they can't believe that there really are Black people out there talented enough to make it to where they are. What they don't know is that any Black person who makes it to this level has had to be so much more talented than the white students and persevere through so much more that getting to this level is in and of itself remarkable.

Advisor: Mary, you're still talking in generalizations that would be true for any person at the graduate level. You're turning this into a racial issue when it really doesn't need to be one.

Me: Alright then, let's go back. You said that I bring this on myself, that no one makes me do these things. Do you really think that I like participating in all of these activities and running around and applying for grants and planning new studies? What enjoyment do you think I get out of this?

Advisor: Well, you say you enjoy what you're doing, and I suppose some part of it is you feeling like you have to do more than everyone else.

Me: I guess you're partly right. But you see, when I get out, I will go into a job that pays me substantially less than what my colleagues of equal qualifications will be paid. These extra activities may help me level the playing field some, but not much. Remember, I said my skin color makes me do this? My skin color will limit how much I make and what I do coming out of graduate school and for the remainder of my life. Essentially my skin color determines the course of my life. The only way for me to fight against this is to work like crazy so I stand out. Unfortunately, my skin color always wins in the end because I can count on someone saying that I got to where I am because I'm Black. That's hard to hear when I know that what really happens is I'll get to where I'm going despite being Black.

Advisor: Well, I think you're making this whole thing up, and I'm going to keep this to show you when you graduate and go into a high-paying job. I really think you paint a much bleaker picture than really exists.

Me: Maybe you are right, and I am a cynic. But one can only live for so long having to prove yourself without internalizing some of what's being thrown at you. You probably have no way of knowing how very frustrating it is to have people assume you are stupid because you are Black, to assume you got ahead because you had an edge. You have no way of knowing how it feels to have to give so much to everyone else that you have nothing left for yourself. You see, white advisor, you don't have to fight against the devils outside who constantly try to hold you down and destroy your very being by telling you that you are worthless because you are Black. More importantly, you don't have to fight against the devils inside of you who are constantly telling you to give up because you are fighting a losing battle and you will never achieve what you deserve, no matter how much you give. You don't have to live with the hurt that I feel every day when I have to prove myself knowing that no matter what I do, it is *never* enough.

Advisor: Have we done something to make you feel like you don't do enough, or do we somehow treat you differently?

Me: It's not one discrete incident that triggers these feelings. You have got to understand that this battle is not something that I fight only when someone pisses me off. I live with this daily. It's not one incident but rather general assumptions like "I want to do as much as I do" that brings the anger to the fore, but the anger is always there. See, you can only fight this battle for so long before you begin to feel the anger, at times an anger so overwhelming that you cannot stand to be around those who have it so easy, those who only have to do what is asked to get ahead. Eventually, you start to feed off this anger, and it becomes your source of energy. A sort of tool to get you ahead. Something you've got that they don't have. I imagine you eventually get to a stage where you accept what is happening around you, you stop being angry, and you play the game without realizing how unfair it is. I don't know that I'll ever reach that point. I don't know that I want to.

So, you see, you say no one makes me do this. Perhaps you are right. But if I didn't do this, I would still be in Kittrell, North Carolina, right now. Although to tell you the truth, sometimes I think it doesn't really matter.

Advisor: Maybe talking to a counselor would be helpful in dealing with this anger you describe. I'm sure a Black clinical psychologist would be available.

Me: You see, that's the problem. I express what happens in my life, nothing atypical for any other Black person in America trying to get ahead, and suddenly, it becomes pathological in some sense. It's not natural to carry around such anger. White people really enjoy saying that. But you know, it's not natural for one group of people to be so empowered and another so disenfranchised that one can make the other feel such anger. But in fact, this anger could actually be a friend to white people. You see, you can only carry it for so long before you burn yourself out. One less threat for the world to worry about. But to answer your question, no, I don't need to talk to a counselor. However, I think I do need to better utilize a network of other Black people who are going through similar experiences. I also think that I need people to not say that what I'm doing is unnecessary or that I bring this stuff on myself. No one would choose to be as tired as I am. Rest assured that what I do is very necessary, and although no one person makes me do it, society wouldn't have it any other way.

I shared this reflection, in writing, with the advisor in 1993 or 1994. To his credit, he did, in fact, keep it. In December 2020, he wrote to me. His email message follows, redacted to ensure his anonymity:

Mary,

I saw your affiliation through ResearchGate. I had not known where you were for all these years. Then, I hesitated to contact you because I wasn't sure how you felt about your years in graduate school and I do not wish to be intrusive or irritating. I'm happy to see your successes, which I know came at great effort and sacrifice.

My only purpose in contacting you is to thank you for having been in my life. Your writing the attached had a profound effect, and I kept the pages on my desk for over 20 years to remind me of what I didn't know and needed to do better. I brought it with me as I retired. I think of you often.

I wish I served you better while in graduate school. In particular, I wish I had been more knowledgeable, understanding, and supportive. I am sure it was tiring and tiresome continually to have to educate others and me of your experience. I know you have continued to have impact in very positive ways—and now as a university president.

I wish you the very best personally and in meeting the challenges of higher education in the pandemic.

I didn't know how to feel about this message. Should I feel grateful that he finally heard some of what I was trying to tell him? He was supposed to be the teacher, and I was supposed to learn from him. I assume that the contact was, in part, precipitated by the high-profile killing of George Floyd and subsequent racial reckoning. I felt a sense of being seen and heard, which was heartening, but I also wondered why it took the death of a Black man and a national outcry for that to happen. Ultimately, I didn't respond, though I will once I find the words.

Early Challenges in the Margins

My marginality didn't end when I earned my PhD. In one of my very first professional positions, I encountered the ways those of us from the margins can make those who are used to being unchallenged in the center feel insecure. In this instance, I was working with a team of people on a major research project and was eager to not only make a positive contribution but to also bring the perspective of those from the margins to those who were studying them. I felt it was important to try to offer a different perspective than those of the researchers. Likewise, I thought it was important to form genuine relationships with our participants, as they were more than mere research subjects to me.

Acting on those urges, and being successful, did not sit well with one team leader who was used to being centered in these conversations. The fact that those we were working with chose to call on me rather than the project lead created tension. The fact that I was successful in my work was also a challenge for this leader.

As a result, this person began to use what will be a familiar strategy to many on the margins. He began to undermine me quietly and privately. When I was traveling for the project, he would call and leave me very long voicemails on the hotel room phone (this predates cell phones) telling me how incompetent I was. In private meetings, he would say that I knew nothing. His mission was to erode my self-esteem to the point that I either believed I was incompetent and gave up or I actually became incompetent due to his harassment and gave up. Ultimately, his goal was to make me quit. This was at a time when phrases like *gaslighting* weren't in common parlance, diversity was just beginning to be discussed in the workplace, and women weren't believed. I did, for longer than I should have, accept this behavior without responding or drawing others' attention to it. When I did draw attention to it, my role on the project was reduced, and I was assigned a different project to work on. He was told not to engage with me and would make a point of turning around and racing away if we encountered one another in the hallway. Interestingly, this strategy of undermining one's confidence and, ultimately, competence, came up again later in my career after I had been established as a leader. And the pattern (on both sides) was the same: the more successful I became, the more personal and vitriolic the attacks were on my work, humanity, and leadership. These attacks, too, were largely kept in the private sphere, though one particular person eventually got very comfortable in their role and would "let them slip" in public venues, as well. Though everyone could hear and know how wrong the comments were, for the sake of harmony, very few people spoke up on my behalf.

And as was the case before, it took me far too long to recognize that I was being actively targeted and undermined. I thought, as many do, that if I just worked harder, things would get better. I thought that I could outwork the harassment. I could not. You cannot. You cannot because the problem isn't the work. The problem is that some people are so deeply threatened by successful people from the margins that the only way they know to respond is to try to tear you down in the most personal, harmful, and secretive ways possible. It is in moments like these that I not only learned the need to advocate for myself, but I also learned the importance of affirming others who find themselves in similar situations, letting them know they aren't imagining it and they aren't alone.

What the Margins Frame

Not only can embracing your marginality help you feel supported and affirmed, but it is also a way to help others in the margins amplify their voices and have their needs met. The first half of my career focused on education from a variety of perspectives: teacher, policy researcher, foundation education program officer, school developer, and adult educator. In several of these roles, my foundation in the margin compelled me to help others hear the voices of those they might normally have ignored. For example, as a school developer, one of my key jobs was partnering with communities to understand their hopes and aspirations for their children's education. While we had educational models to deploy, it was important to recognize that those models needed to resonate and stem from those in the community being served. While I did not perceive it in this way at the time, I strayed from the leadership norm when I prioritized asking questions, carefully listening to responses, respecting what was heard, and building our programs and policies accordingly. I privileged these steps because I, like our research community, was from the margins. Without question, asking, listening, respecting, and partnering with communities makes the process longer and more complex; however, it also yields a better product and ensures that those with the most at stake are heard and centered. Being from the margins helped me to have that insight, which I hope allowed me to perform my job and serve my community better.

A similar lesson was learned when I worked with adult learners, in this case, entrepreneurs from marginalized communities who were seeking support in building their businesses. I had the honor of working with Walter Geier, someone who taught me that when one is invited into a community, your perspective is to be one of a curious learner. In fact, the entire curriculum we utilized was premised on helping these burgeoning entrepreneurs understand their own aspirations and potential, as well as how they could build a business plan to support bringing those goals to fruition. Our stance was not to judge but to coach and encourage. Again, while my thinking at the time was not that my being from the margins called me to and framed this work, it is clear now that it was a powerful factor.

From my earliest professional positions, my career took me to several educational nonprofits and then into higher education, with leadership roles in student affairs, strategic planning, diversity and equity, and, finally, academic affairs. Throughout, my origin in the margins was present in my work.

Routinely throughout my career, the question of who can, does, and should have access to higher education has arisen. Many assume the answer to the question is that all students can access a college education. This is a fraught assumption. Higher education in the United States was transported from Europe and was a system that served to control which social classes had access to knowledge and the opportunity to contribute to the generation of knowledge.

At some point, perhaps with greater access to K-12 education, the assumption was born that higher education is for all. Yet the original model of higher education and its exclusive structures and traditions have been steadfast even though the landscape of higher education dramatically shifted. The higher education paradigm works very well for those who inherit the legacy of a college education.

But as the demographics of those who comprise colleges shift, there has been no move to make the culture more inclusive.

Rather, the student must fit our narrow cultural norms. This paradox is difficult to negotiate for those of us whose work involves diversity. Additionally, it is difficult to negotiate for those of us who don't fit the narrow cultural norms of higher education ourselves.

Philosophically, we are marching toward expanding opportunities for underrepresented populations. Historically, however, higher education is securely grounded in granting limited and exclusive access to the system. How do we reconcile this new movement and a centuries-old system?

There has been significant discussion surrounding why racial discrepancies in outcomes and graduation rates exist. The consensus by some is that students of color don't fit into the higher education culture (the same is also said of highly trained, academically credentialed faculty of color and leaders who come from the margins). However, the question needs to be reshaped to ask how could, and should, higher education be realigned to support all students, not just those few it was originally designed to serve. Given its history, higher education is what is unprepared in this equation, not students.

Leaders from the margins can play an impactful role in identifying, calling out, and reconfiguring colleges and universities to be inclusive and supportive of diverse students. We can explore those time-honored practices, rituals, and traditions that are exclusionary and hinder students from learning, such as utilizing curricula and pedagogical methods that have no resonance with students. We can fashion higher education to meet the needs of the students who are there as opposed to the, supposedly, idyllic students of days gone by. We can stop trying to fit students to match a system that was never created for them and was, in fact, intended to discard or constrain them.

Without this transformational leadership, we are likely to continue to see large disparities between students because they are having largely disparate experiences. If we fail to rethink higher education, where it works and where it does not, we will continue to replicate its inequities in increasing proportions. The following chapters explore the ways that my identity elements—in the margins—continue to play a significant role in how I lead, how my leadership is perceived by others, and the educational environments in which I lead.

Questions for Reflection

- Who are the costars in your life story? Why? What lessons—positive or negative—can you reflect on to encourage you today?
- When we each decided to become a leader, we committed to sharing our stories. How can you share your story to inspire another?
- How can you listen to someone else's story with an open heart? How can you use your open heart to encourage them?

CHAPTER 3

Leading While Black

HEADLINE: College of Saint Benedict Appoints First Black President

Being named a college president is truly an honor. The move into such a role reflects years of hard work and sacrifice, and a commitment to continued hard work and sacrifice ahead. Yet as I approach nearly a decade of being a college president, I continue to wonder how I "should" have felt about the announcement of my first presidency focusing on my race. I share with you my wonderings because they reflect the type of internal wrestling that leaders from the margins must constantly engage with.

On the one hand, I am unapologetically proud to be the first Black president of two institutions of higher education. I am clear—and openly share with others—that like every person, my race has shaped my being, my experiences, and my leadership. There is no question about that. At the same time, however, there are moments when the headline is something of a dog whistle, a subtle indication that my race either helped me attain the job or will impact the ability with which I will do the job.

I have never seen a white president's race listed in a leadership announcement. No one automatically assumes that a white president's race is central to their leadership, and it feels unfair to make that assumption about leaders of color. Whether read positively or negatively, the added notation singles my leadership out as different and, for some, less than.

To truly understand how to embrace race as a valuable component of my marginality and my leadership, it is important to understand how leaders experience, engage, and address race in their work. In this moment of racial reckoning, the sheer number of articles about and general interest in developing leaders of color is heartening. In many ways, it seems as if the struggles of leaders of color are finally being recognized and, perhaps overly optimistically, addressed. However, despite the current conversation, my leadership—and the behaviors of those with whom I lead—were not solely developed post–2020's racial reckoning. It is critically important to understand the context of 2020 and what led to that moment for leaders to understand how race shapes one's leadership in the margins.

Race and Leadership: A Primer

Leadership literature within higher education and in the corporate sector most often highlights three themes in the study of the leadership practice of successful Black leaders: the need to outperform, the need to be resilient, and the desire to serve a community. My personal narrative shared in the prior chapter certainly speaks to these aspects. But let's look a bit closer at the wider research on race and leadership.

There is an often-shared adage that leaders of color must work twice as hard as white leaders to be successful. Research also finds that leaders of color work harder for fewer rewards. A 2007 study of African American female college and university presidents found that "minority women CEOs consistently selected 'exceeding performance expectations' as their primary strategy for navigating obstacles . . . [and] in obtaining the presidency."[1] The study went on to note that these leaders "strive for excellence and refuse to let the pressures of race and gender discrimination prevent them from attaining their goals. African-American female presidents have capitalized on their strengths, recognized their weaknesses, sought leadership training and upgraded their educational skills. Equipped with positive attitudes and tenacity in the face of adversity, these women turned challenges into opportunities."[2] The need for enhanced performance for those from the margins is coupled with the need for great perseverance.

Studies of leadership in the corporate sector echoed the need for Black leaders to exceed expectations and exhibit uncommon resilience. For example, a 2019 report on senior Black leaders in corporate America concluded that:

> The pressure is high on Black leaders. There's a prevailing belief in corporate America that Black leaders are promoted because of their race, not because of their qualifications and capabilities. That makes it much harder for Black leaders to be seen and appreciated. So that's why so many are under pressure. In fact, 57 percent of the Black leaders in our study reported having to work twice as hard and needing to accomplish twice as much as their peers to be viewed as on the same level. . . . The case is even more dire for Black women, as they are members of two underrepresented groups. . . .

[Further, t]he Black leaders in our study are resilient. For 90 percent of these leaders, setbacks serve to motivate them more, and they handle adversity with maturity and grace. That's true even though 50 percent of the Black leaders in our study have confronted unfair treatment and microaggressions, such as being mistaken for their white counterpart's subordinate, when it was the other way around. Guided by their belief system, whether grounded in their faith or their passion for their organization's mission and vision, they were inspired to persevere and continue looking and moving forward.[3]

Another example: In 2018, on the fiftieth anniversary of the founding of the African-American Student Union at Harvard Business School, *Harvard Business Review* reported on a study of 67 African American women who graduated between 1977 and 2015 and attained chief executive leadership roles.[4] In analyzing the career paths of these 67 Black women, the authors identified a need to outperform in order to succeed: "Certainly, they are well prepared and highly competitive in the job market; according to our data, they have invested more years in higher education, at more-selective institutions, than their colleagues and their non-African-American classmates." But, the report also concluded that resilience is equally important:

In simple terms, the answer to the question of what it takes to succeed can be reduced to a single capacity: resilience. To be sure, resilience has been widely celebrated as a character virtue in the past decade, and it plays a role in every success narrative, regardless of a person's race or gender. But the African-American women we interviewed seemed to rely more heavily than others on that quality, because of the frequency with which they encountered obstacles and setbacks resulting from the intersecting dynamics of race, gender, and other identities. In each case they bounced back, refused to get distracted or derailed, and maintained forward progress.

The need to outperform colleagues and to be resilient in the face of explicit and implicit racism is a key leadership strength for Black leaders. These are among the most valuable lessons and the greatest strengths those on the margins bring with them. When you dwell in spaces where others cannot see you, when your needs are ignored and your hopes diminished, you learn how to navigate in such a way to be seen, even when that navigation unfairly demands more from you. Likewise, dwelling in the margins—especially when one's marginality includes poverty—means being and creating resilience in one's life. It means constantly overcoming setbacks as you begin your life's race from somewhere off the track.

Therefore, I believe that leaders of color feel the added opportunity, and necessity, to give back through their leadership. In my inauguration address at Hollins University, I described this desire to give back, often reflected in one being the "first," as both a burden and a joy:

> You see, sometimes the price for success means being the first. I know what it is to feel the burden of being the unimaginable first. The burden of being doubted. The burden of being perceived as less than. The burden of the call to be more. The burden of a world telling you you are not enough. However, when I hug a student and offer encouragement, or see tears in the eyes of an alumna of color, I find a powerful reminder of the joy one can feel when one answers the call of leadership. In addition to the burden, there is also joy in being first; there is joy in supporting others because you and they are, in fact, enough; there is joy in taking those initial steps despite so many more steps ahead.

This dialectic of burden and joy is rife throughout the experiences of leaders from the margins. For leaders from the margins, the need to be successful is not only for themselves, but also for the sake of others in the margins.

A study published in 2017 speaks to the unique phenomenon among African American graduate students to pursue a PhD with the explicit goal of giving back to a community. Author Carmen McCallum finds factors driving the pursuit of doctoral credentials: honoring a commitment, breaking barriers and increasing pathways, infiltrating conversations, and giving back to one's community.[5] These desires directly reflect the impact of being in the margins for many Black Americans and how their race has shaped how they think about their leadership. McCallum writes:

> The majority of participants focused on how earning the degree would assist them in giving back to African Americans as a group but a few specifically discussed their desire to give back to *their* community—the community or hometown they left in order to pursue their academic dreams. These participants viewed their leaving home as a community sacrifice. It meant one less person was in the community working toward its improvement. Because the community was willing to sacrifice and "let them go off to college," participants felt obligated to return the gesture by returning to the community and instigating change.[6]

These motivations for doctoral credentials indicate that, from a racialized perspective, although one can travel from the margins to the center, the calling to return to the margins is significant and meritorious.

Others' Perceptions of Your Leadership
as a Person of Color

Each of the studies above looked at how Black leaders view and understand their own leadership. While the development of these skills is essential to being a successful leader, as a leader from the margins, you are still confronted with others' perceptions of your leadership. Even when a leader of color exhibits exemplary outperformance, resilience, and commitment to community, they confront challenges to their position as a leader. For some in the center, it is just that unthinkable that an individual from the margins can successfully lead. Instead, your leadership becomes tokenizing or symbolic, with others ignoring the pressure and effort expended to excel.

Despite our work ethic or resilience, we are often confronted with being viewed as little more than racialized figureheads. Being labeled a "Black president" is also tokenizing. Research shows that many people presume that minority women experience subtle race and gender discrimination from higher education colleagues and students and, regardless of qualifications, are often perceived as tokens.[7] This notion makes it even more difficult as a leader.

Additionally, a Black president is too often seen as a symbol—a symbol that a community has eradicated racism. A symbol that a campus has moved on from past wrongs. A symbol that justice has been achieved and that anti-racist work is done. This symbol is false, and it is sometimes used to replace (or ignore) the real, ongoing work that needs to be done to become an inclusive, anti-racist community, and to support a leader of color.

As a woman of color, daily I must confront many preconceptions about my level of intelligence, how I attained my current position, my ability to think complexly about issues beyond race, and my willingness to nurture all the students I serve, not just students of color. When I use my authentic voice as a Black woman, I am often challenged, as that somehow feels threatening to others. Here's what I mean: The value attached to leadership from the margins can be destabilizing—threatening—for the entire organization. A study of top executives at US companies found that the appointment of a female or racial minority CEO diminished white male managers' sense of identification with their company.[8] Leaders from the margins are viewed as a compromise for others, even though the real risk is the fragile egos of those used to being unquestioned in the center.

To combat these perceptions, many leaders from the margins feel forced to contort themselves and prove their value to those in the center. They work to fulfill the expectations of others, rather than having the opportunity to focus on self-understanding and authentic leadership. Tokenizing and symbolism usurp the reality that being a leader from the margins offers its own value.

In the early 2020s, there are many challenging leadership issues for college presidents, including an essential, ongoing, and painful racial reckoning. For many white individuals, this period revealed for the first time racist systems and actions that have been long evident to people of color in America. Those noticing injustice as a new phenomenon often have expectations about an urgent response that are different from the expectations of those who have been battling injustice from the margins since birth. For example, the notion of writing statements about national events is fraught for all college presidents, especially when dealing with issues of race. That complication is only enhanced when the president is a person of color. There are moments, for example following the murder of George Floyd, when I simply could not be silent—I had to use my platform to react, to respond, and to comfort. But there have been other moments when the public response served only to remind me that my experience, as a leader of color, a leader from the margins, was often very different than those of the people I had the privilege of leading.

These inflection points reinforce for me the importance of honoring one's own journey as a person of color and not allowing it to be circumscribed by others. The consistent exposure to and navigation around structural racism for leaders from the margins creates a resilience that can positively impact one's ability to lead. At the same time, that constant navigation exhausts the mind, body, and spirit. While a leadership role absolutely affords one some privilege, systemic structures never allow you to forget the fragility of that privilege. Finding a way to dwell in the tension between what my leadership demands and what my heart feels is a constant and dynamic process—a process I talk openly about because it's important to support others in the margins by acknowledging the experience and to let those in the center know that those of us who are marginalized are human beings, not just headlines.

What the Margins Frame

As a person of color from the margins, I have learned that while I am responsible for my leadership, I am also subject to others' assumptions about what it means to be a leader of color. The margins have helped me learn how to not be stalled by those assumptions. In fact, because of my experiences in the margins, I have found that my leadership is an important source of support for students and faculty of color. I recall a conversation among college leaders who shared that no matter your race or gender, you are everyone's president. That is surely true. However, everyone's president is a woman of color when I am that leader. This means that groups that have historically been unseen or undervalued are now visible. It also means that those in the center have a new experience of engaging with the margins and those who hail from them.

Being a leader of color is also important as we think about institutional change. In chapter seven, I will discuss how race can play a role in institutional transformation. Whether at the institutional or personal level, being a leader of color from the margins represents a great deal. My presence in rooms wherein I am the only person or woman of color represents defiance or transgression in a room of otherwise white leaders. I am equipped for this, having previously found myself in these situations and developed the needed leadership skills to navigate these spaces. Being from the margins also provides me with the courage to talk about how these rooms need to change.

The ability to both persevere and call for change comes from having learned in the margins to rely on our own leadership compasses. While others may discount the value of the margins, recognizing, accepting, and embracing our marginality makes it easier to trust our own leadership and support the leadership development of others.

Finally, it is important to note that while this chapter focused on race, it is impossible to separate the impact of my race on my leadership from the impact of gender. These intersecting identities are critically important to both my marginality and my leadership. In the next chapter, I consider the collision of gender and race in my leadership journey.

Questions for Reflection

- How has your race impacted your leadership?
- How has racial privilege opened opportunities for you? What did you learn in those moments?
- How has racism foreclosed opportunities for you? What did you learn in those moments?
- Can you and do you openly address race as part of your leadership platform? Why or why not?
- How can the perseverance and grit you have developed help sustain your leadership?
- How can your racialized experiences amplify your leadership? What must you guard against?
- What have you been taught or exposed to in the margins about race that you need to let go?

CHAPTER 4

Leading While Female

In theory, the challenges that leaders of color face might be easy to separate from those that women experience, but it is the intersection of those identities that is the lived experience of a leader. For women, the leadership imperative is clear.

In the United States, women make up 57 percent of higher education students and earn more than 50 percent of degrees at most higher education levels.[1] Compare those numbers to faculty, of which women only make up 31 percent.[2] Women are more common in administrative roles, holding more than 50 percent of such positions. However, a woman's journey up the organizational chart dramatically narrows, with only 40 percent of senior positions (cabinet-level) held by women. Only 30 percent of college presidents are women. Of course, when we overlay additional identities, in this instance race, the numbers are even

This chapter is adapted from Mary Dana Hinton, "The Genuine Authenticity It Takes to Lead," in *Thriving as a Woman in Leadership in Higher Education: Stories and Strategies from Your Peers*, ed. Elizabeth Ross Hubbell and Daniel Fusch (Denver: Academic Impressions, 2021), 9–19. Used with permission.

more disheartening. Overall, women of color comprise less than 10 percent of the higher education workforce and hold only 5 percent of college presidencies.[3] The data makes a clear and compelling case for women's leadership development.

Several questions immediately arise from these numbers: Is there something unique about being a woman in higher education? What does leadership mean, for women and for women in higher education? What are the barriers women face in our sector? What strengths and opportunities should we be utilizing and leveraging in higher education as women and as leaders? What skills do we need to develop and enhance? Are there women whose background might seem like a deficit when, in reality, their background is their greatest strength? And how do gender and race collide to complicate these matters even more?

According to an article in *Forbes*:

> While both white and black women face potential lose/lose double binds, black women's double bind is far more precarious than that of white women's. If white women are seen as too communal to lead, they will still be seen as likable, but black women lose either way: if they are seen as angry they are unlikable; if they are seen as subservient they are not respected. In other words, black women must navigate *their* lose/lose dilemma in such a way that they get it *just right* or they will be seen as neither leaders nor likable.[4]

This double bind is a real challenge that women of color face as leaders, a challenge that can derail their leadership and their personhood. As a study of Black women leaders in higher education noted: "As African Americans, they are subject to the racism that has been part of the American experience. As women, they are subjected to the sexism that women face in the larger population. However, much of the work that takes place on race in the United States ignores the role of gender, and much of the feminist critique of society ignores race."[5] Leaders from the margins are susceptible to these challenges but also have the unique skills to address and change them. In this chapter, I will explore what the data show about women in leadership roles and the ways experiences in the margins help equip one for success.

Women's Leadership: A Primer

A quick Google search of the phrase "women's leadership"* yields many articles about the value of women's leadership. In each, we are told how to capitalize on our innate leadership skills. Finally, it seems, traditionally feminine leadership skills are valued—those exact skills that so many of us have developed as we operated within a "man's world." The words resilience, authenticity, team, and communicator continuously arise when women's leadership is described.

Existing research on women in leadership—coming from various geographies and disciplines including business, psychology, sociology, and education—is vast. Historical literature tended to focus on women's leadership styles or characteristic ways of behaving (often in comparison to men's styles or ways of behaving).[6] These studies of women's leadership often included only white, middle-class, heterosexual women and did not illuminate the way that the intersectionality of these

---

* Identity is both self-defined and imposed upon you by others. While gender is not a binary, women and men are often treated within our society as a dichotomy, and the leadership literature often differentiates women's and men's ways of leading. My own experience as a cisgender woman leading in women's college contexts both reflects the binary and makes visible the multitude of ways that people who identify as women engage with the world.

women's racial/ethnic, class, and sexual identities affect their leadership. Generalizations about women's leadership styles tend to promote an essentialized view of women's leadership, normalizing a universal standard of women.[7] And, advice to women leaders too often is relevant primarily to women with other forms of privilege: "Lean in," they say.[8] "Know your value."[9]

In the margins, I find that leadership advice unhelpful, as it maintains a center to which women must ascribe, as opposed to embracing what the margins offer. I believe that a singular "women's way of leading" is a fallacy, and I am much more interested in the ways that diverse women's leadership is perceived and valued.

In gendered workplaces, leaders are stereotypically seen as agentic: confident, competent, decisive, forceful, and independent. Men are stereotypically seen in precisely the same ways. Consequently, men are regarded as natural leaders, but women—both Black and white—must overcome serious challenges to be seen as competent, confident leaders. White women are stereotypically seen as communal: pleasant, caring, deferential, and concerned about others.[10] Their leadership challenge, therefore, is to avoid being seen as so communal as to be an ineffective leader without being seen as so agentic as to be unlikable. Black women face a very different challenge. They are not stereotypically seen as communal but rather as assertive, angry, and "having an attitude." Their challenge, therefore, is to avoid being seen as so angry or assertive as to be unlikable without being seen as so subservient and compliant as to be lacking in strength and independence.[11] Therefore, while I will never deny the challenges white women face in the world—they are many—I also know that the challenges I face are different and compounded by the intersection of race and gender.

I like to think we are at a moment when we realize that those things that once placed us in a stark contrast to what was previously perceived as good (read: male) leadership qualities are now viewed as advantages. Because, while some of these traits were historically viewed as signs of weakness, I think they hold within them the greatest power of leadership. That said, in some ways the concept of "women's leadership" still threatens to homogenize the multifaceted ways that women successfully practice leadership—for example, as natural collaborators, or natural consensus-builders, or natural servant-leaders—setting up a false dichotomy that suggests we aren't decisive, or forthright, or assertive. I encourage you to think through your own leadership characteristics, as defined solely by you, and to imagine how you can leverage your unique characteristics to excel as a leader. For myself, it's knowing and leveraging my authentic strengths and understanding my identities—especially in the margins—that best serve my leadership.

Yet rising to leadership roles as women is often fraught. Shelley Correll and her colleagues have conducted extensive research on the role of performance evaluations in revealing gender bias that illuminates how women's leadership is perceived:

> In summary, we find that managers did not view men and women differently on the dimension of taking charge, but they did value taking charge more for men than for women. Importantly, this "valuing but not viewing" pattern for taking charge was opposite of the pattern found for being helpful. We found that managers viewed women as more helpful, but there was no gender difference in how they valued helpfulness. Putting the two findings together, we see how the combined effects of viewing and valuing differences can lead to novel patterns of gender disadvantage for

women. Women were viewed as more helpful, but helpfulness was not associated with the highest ratings that directly affect compensation and promotion opportunities. Women tech workers were viewed as equally likely to "take charge" as their men counterparts, but this set of behaviors was only associated with the highest ratings when enacted by men.[12]

Additionally, over the past several years we have begun to note that women and people of color are finding themselves in leadership roles with a higher propensity for failure. We are finding more women facing what is known as the "glass cliff," a term that was first named in 2005:

[I]t appears that women are particularly likely to be placed in positions of leadership in circumstances of general financial downturn and downturn in company performance. In this way, such women can be seen to be placed on top of a "glass cliff," in the sense that their leadership appointments are made in problematic organizational circumstances and hence are more precarious. . . .

It is already well established that women face greater challenges than men in their attempts to climb to the top of the corporate ladder. Moreover, it is apparent that even if they arrive there, women are likely to receive greater scrutiny and criticism than men, and to secure less positive evaluations, even when performing exactly the same leadership roles. It now seems apparent that in addition to obstacles, the leadership positions that women occupy are likely to be less promising than those of their male counterparts. So, in addition to confronting a glass ceiling and not having access to a glass elevator, they are also likely to be placed on a glass cliff.[13]

Ryan and Haslam's groundbreaking study shows that women are granted unequal opportunity even when granted an opportunity. And, as with most issues, we see this phenomenon playing out unequally with leaders of color, too:

Even when Black leaders break through the glass ceiling, they often find themselves standing on a "glass cliff"—facing a high-risk assignment where few can succeed. More than a third (36 percent) of Black leaders we spoke with said they were given tough projects that no one else wanted to handle. And the unspoken assumption was that they were given these projects so they could prove their worth. While experiences like these can build skills and credibility, Black leaders reported finding themselves in this situation a disproportionate number of times compared to their white peers. This practice demoralizes Black talent, so they may leave the organization, depleting the leadership pipeline of valuable talent and skills.[14]

There is no "women's way of leading," but gender is, without a doubt, a contributing factor in *how* one leads. Reimagined this way, especially if one tosses aside the binary understanding of gender, we arrive at a place where we can argue that gender matters and it shapes leadership (and how leaders are perceived), but the pathways and specific experiences of *individuals* matter. And—even more exciting, I think—we can make the argument that all of this unfolds in a *dynamic, ongoing landscape*. We are shaped by experiences and history and circumstances, but we are not molded by these forces into a fixed, final form. We are fluid, and experiences and history and circumstances *continue to act upon and shape leaders*. Some aspects of your leadership style (and how you are perceived) will be in place when you begin your career. And some of these qualities will persist throughout your career. But as your work unfolds, not only will you learn and develop, but external forces, history, and circumstances will continue to shape you and shape how you are perceived.

What the Margins Frame

Therefore, it is clear that women in the margins face multiple and unique challenges. It is for another author to trace fully the history of women's leadership theory. It is my task here, however, to proclaim that those young people on the margins who grow up seeing strong women can and are positively impacted by those role models. For those of us who grew up in those communities, we see something uniquely special about women's voices and the need to promote and support those voices. Likewise, you will find a strong commitment to women's agency among marginalized communities.

You'll recall that in my childhood community, many households were headed by some such women as single parents. Due to my father's death when I was 10, I, too, was raised by a single mother. I lived in a world of women: aunts, cousins, fictive kin, "church mothers," and women neighbors who played an outsize role in developing my sense of self. In our community, these women worked outside the home, provided for their families, tended the children, quietly ran the churches, and more. These women showed me daily that women were, in fact, leaders. They ruled my world, and while there were men present—men who were held out publicly as "the" leaders—it was abundantly clear who wielded power in the community.

Like many young Black girls, I was explicitly taught to never rely on a man and to always have my own money. Some would argue that these lessons are more gender- than race-based, but for me, it was impossible to separate the two. The deep harms and burdens placed on Black men—who are often depicted and treated as less than human, inherently violent, and devoid of love—caused harm to the entire community. The wider world exerted these pressures on the community, which resulted in women having to be strong and sustain one another, men, and children. One can trace this reality back to enslavement when Black men and women were not legally allowed to marry and were separated at the whim of slave owners. This enforced lack of stability has long consequences and the trauma it exerted on Black families is an unwanted legacy.

As a result, growing up in the margins taught me a depth of self-sufficiency that promotes strong leadership. I understood that I had to work hard, outperform, merely to survive. On the other hand, in full disclosure, I also developed a resistance to asking for help that I have had to work hard to outgrow. Leaders from the margins today need to both embrace initiative and learn to ask for help in order to thrive.

I also grew up with the assumption that women were in charge. However, I was always aware of and bothered by the fact that women were not allowed to publicly embrace their power. In many ways, it was the community of Black women I grew up with—and my desire to push back on the prevailing notion that women's power is to be hidden—who imbued in me a strong sense of what it means to be a leader and a desire to become one. However, in the world outside of my own, it was challenging to find women in leadership roles, and I soon learned that few valued women's leadership in the same way I did, and that, in fact, women were viewed as less than when it came to leadership. However, dwelling in the margins provided me with the opportunity to see the ways women wielded power implicitly.

And though I believe and am committed to helping women own their voices and power, watching the ways women navigated power in the face of tradition provided me with important models for leadership.

Generational Impact

It is important for me to acknowledge that my understanding and experience of gender are also mediated by my generation. As someone who came of age in the era of Murphy Brown and Cagney and Lacey, and in the shadow of *Julia*, starring Diahann Carroll (the first Black woman to have her own series), it was clear that women had the capacity and potential to care for themselves and exact agency over their own lives. A child of the 1970s, it was also made clear that to be successful as a woman, you actually needed to try to be a man. For example, in "African-American Female College Presidents: Self Conceptions of Leadership," Anna Waring explains:

> Early books on women managers, such as *The Managerial Woman* (1976) and *Games Mother Never Taught You* (1977) stressed that if women were to succeed, they needed to learn to play the game the way men do. Strategies suggested that women learn to model their behavior and expectations on that of males, especially their male bosses. The military model of hierarchy and the sports model of being one of the team provide the context for advising women how to behave in corporate settings.[15]

This notion that women should simply be men in order to lead heavily shaped my own understanding of leadership. I grew up among a generation of women who were told that some things are completely out of the realm of possibility if you want to be a successful woman. First, whatever you do, never show emotion in the workplace. Authenticity and vulnerability were explicitly viewed as anathema to being a good leader. For a few generations, we were told to separate our personal lives from our professional lives. We were also told that we had to both act and dress like men to be successful and accepted as leaders. A 1990s study, released around the time I began my professional career, found that "applicants were perceived as more forceful, aggressive and so on when wearing more masculine clothing. Applicants also received more favorable hiring recommendations when wearing more masculine clothing."[16] If you chose to pay attention to something as frivolous as your appearance, or didn't learn to play golf, or took time off to go on a field trip with your child, it was perceived as proof that you were not a leader.

Ultimately, we were told that we must choose either work or motherhood, and structures were created that enforced the choice to have a career or a family. And, we were told to apologize for whatever choice we made. Early and often, apologize. We were told to feel guilty if we chose to work (*How selfish, you're not a real woman if you don't have kids!*) and guilty if we chose to stay home (*I thought you were a feminist!*) Most of us quietly decided we would try to have both and learned to apologize for that, too. How many nights have we felt we failed our children? That number is likely only matched by the number of nights we felt we failed our career. Yet most of all, when we spend our nights feeling like failures, we are failing ourselves.

In this context, certainly many women freely choose to leave the world of work, but many are also forced out, either because of narrowly defined expectations of what it means to be a leader, familial circumstances, or because they simply do not have the structural support—in the office or at home—to enable them to thrive. During and following the COVID-19 pandemic, women left the workforce because they were more likely to have jobs in industries that were shut down or severely impacted, with women making up 54 percent of the job losses. Women were less likely to be able to work from home than men (22 percent of women compared to 28 percent of men). But the biggest impact is the need for childcare, which has driven women out of the workforce at high levels and has compromised women's earnings now and well into the future, including their retirement. "One out of four women who reported becoming unemployed during the pandemic said it was because of a lack of childcare—twice the rate among men."[17] And, it has increased the burden on women for unpaid work in the home, compromising their ability to work, with 10 percent saying their work is impacted weekly.

As women and as leaders, how do we take back that conversation and determine what we want for ourselves at this moment in time?

What the Margins Frame

The margins have taught me, as a woman, how to navigate and wield power in ways that those in the center may not have developed. This flexible approach has helped me develop a number of ways to lead, ways that may not have been as readily accessible in the center.

Similarly, for women, there is a broad conversation about the many lose/lose propositions we face in the margins. To know that we are more likely to be invited into leadership positions on the glass cliff means that we know we must conduct intense due diligence and be much more mindful about leadership opportunities presented to us before we accept them. Being in the margins equips us to observe and ask questions.

Finally, because women are often placed in unwinnable positions ("Don't be too motherly!" "Don't be too harsh!"), as with race, women in the margins have permission to let their authentic voice emerge, as opposed to expending tremendous energy attempting to fight an unwinnable battle. Being in the margins grants the permission needed to not play the same games that are played in the center.

Questions for Reflection

- What was your generation taught about women and leadership?
- How has your own leadership been framed around those implicit understandings?
- What is your definition of having it "all"? How are you working toward it?
- How will you know when you have achieved your "all"?
- What role do your various identities play in understanding "all"?

CHAPTER 5

Navigating toward Leadership from the Rural South

All people have intersecting identities that they carry with them in all situations. I understand identity as "a self-concept, in part self- and in part socially constructed, always in response to the limitations of what is acceptable."[1] Lumby suggested that the multiple identities that affect women's leadership are broader than the "usual" categories (gender, race/ethnicity, sexuality, disability, and age). She concluded that the impact of gender on leadership "cannot be understood fully without taking account of the metamorphosis of gender as it collides with, permeates and transmutes in the presence of other identities."[2]

It is important for me to acknowledge the role my rural upbringing played in shaping my leadership and life on the margins. While conversations about diversity and inclusion are common on many college campuses and in most academic spheres, the focus tends to be on certain aspects of identity over others: racial and ethnic diversity, and diversity of sexual orientation and gender identity are often the focus. Other identities that play a role in people's experiences in higher education, such as geographic identity and class identity, are less often studied.

As someone from the rural South, however, the impact of these identities is obvious in my own narrative. Evidence of a rural consciousness is available beyond my experience as well. The 2016 US presidential election illustrated the importance of geographic identity and the divide between rural and urban communities in the United States. The differences in political views are linked to differing social status, sociocultural values and beliefs, and attitudes toward domestic social issues for urban and rural residents.[3] Katherine J. Cramer's 2016 book describes a sense of place-based resentment in rural areas rooted in three elements:

> (1) a belief that rural areas are ignored by decision makers, including policy makers, (2) a perception that rural areas do not get their fair share of resources, and (3) a sense that rural folks have fundamentally distinct values and lifestyles, which are misunderstood and disrespected by city folks.[4]

According to Cramer, the result is a deep divide characterized by the fact that those who live in rural communities "prefer lifestyles that differ fundamentally from those of city people."[5] Beliefs about race, social class, fairness, and justice play into this divide.

Colleges and universities are widely perceived as falling on the urban—and liberal—side of this divide. Enke and Zenk summarized this phenomenon in 2019:

> Nearly 90 percent of U.S. college students go to college in metropolitan areas with more than 100,000 people, and more than half go to college in the 52 metros with more than one million inhabitants (Florida, 2016). And, in general, higher education

institutions are seen as politically liberal places, with six in ten faculty members at all baccalaureate institutions in the United States characterizing their own political views as "far left" or "liberal" (Eagan et al., 2014). In contrast, less than 13 percent of faculty members described their political views as "far right" or "conservative."[6]

It is in this climate that I consider my own leadership, as a leader raised in the rural South. At the time and place in which I was born, the notion of complex identities also frames the margins themselves. Before talking about class and rurality, let's take a step back and explore how identities have been used to shape the margins.

How the Margins Are Defined by Those in the Center

To relegate people to the margins and make them feel less than in that space, it is important that discord is generated among those in the margins, in part to keep them from pursuing the center. This "divide and rule" tactic has been deployed by colonizers and victors throughout history: In 146 BCE, the longstanding Achaean League of Greek city states dissolved when the Romans treated the various states differently. The Ottoman Empire often used a divide and rule strategy to expand their power, pitting Armenians and Kurds against one another. Animosity between Hindus and Muslims in India increased notably when the British Raj began to artificially engineer conflict to solidify its rule. And, in the early 1930s, Belgian colonizers cemented the ethno-racial classifications of Rwandans as Hutu, Tutsi, and Twa, and reshaped and mythologized the ethnic identities in ways that provided the basis for genocide.

To keep people on the margins, and to keep those same people questioning their value, requires a careful social construct, seemingly perpetuated by those in the center. Malcolm X described how the divide and conquer strategy employed by colonizers was also used against Black people in America. "She [America] makes us think we have different objectives, different goals."[7] By ensuring that low-income whites and Blacks were fighting one another, and that Black people were fighting among themselves, the battleground became the margins and the center remained secure and undisturbed. This practice was seen throughout the southern United States from the time of enslavement through the mid to late twentieth century.[8] This prevented marginalized groups from seeking equity with the center. Further, the idea that one could build community within the margins and use that community to lift others did not feel like an option. This pattern was destructive for all who were subject to it, both collectively and independently.

There were moments when my greatest battle on the margins was with others in the margins. As an adolescent, I became aware that, as a woman of color in the rural South, it was unlikely that my academic aspirations and potential would be carefully nurtured. That was reserved for middle- and upper-class white students. I gained this insight from my Black compatriots, who reminded me constantly that I was chasing an unattainable dream and that I, and my aspirations, "sounded" white. Sounding white had limited utility in our world. I could sound as white as I liked, and I was still bound by my race. Sounding white in the 1980s in North Carolina only sent a confusing signal to whites and a suspicious signal to Blacks. (I admit, the yearbook quote that went viral in 2017 holds a special place in my heart, though the premise wasn't as true in 1988. In the words of Savanna

Tomlinson: "Anything is possible when you sound Caucasian on the phone."[9])

As an adolescent, I was left feeling like I existed on an island. The rationale among my Black peers that hard work is not equal to success was a real (and arguably correct) one in post–Jim Crow North Carolina. Where would intellectual investment get me? Where could it get me? Into a factory job where I would be paid less than my white co-workers? My Black colleagues were incredibly realistic about the challenges inherent in my academic pursuit. And yet, I wanted to be taken seriously for my mind. My goal, like so many of the students we serve today, was access to opportunities that others may not have chosen to avail themselves of but opportunities that could lead to something great for my family and me. The bind I, and many today, faced was from all sides. My response: Defy everyone! I would defy the limitations that my Black peers saw for me by continuing to work hard for more, especially more intellectually. I would defy the limited expectations of the white community for my achievement as a Black woman. It wasn't that I aspired to be white; it was that I aspired to have the opportunity white students had.

Those on the margins aren't valued and, in response, often don't fully claim the marginal space as their own. This was powerfully taught to me as a young person in the rural South. While it would be less than truthful to intimate that I owned that space as an adolescent, what I realize, in hindsight, is that creating environments wherein young people can, with pride and integrity, own that margin is invaluable. It took most of my professional career to realize that by owning that space, I was not only elevating my own ideals and mission, but I was also giving permission to others on the margins to do the same. My return to the South as the president of Hollins University is, in many ways, my way of once again attempting to defy those who suggest that the margins lack value or that those from rural or exurban areas lack value. That said, rurality and class can draw powerful margins.

Socioeconomics in the Rural South

The identity of the rural South is also often deeply linked to class identity. Poverty rates are higher in rural counties than in metropolitan counties, contributing to challenges with health, housing, crime, education, and employment in rural communities.[10] We also know that growing up in poverty, with class as a margin, impacts opportunity. According to Curt and Anne Dudley-Marling, "the categories of race, gender, language, and disability frequently overlap with poverty. No one is ever *just* poor. People living in poverty are also raced, classed, and gendered, speak a particular language, and are members of ethnic and cultural groups. Notably, Black Americans, women, second language learners, and people with disabilities are disproportionately represented among children and adults living in poverty."[11]

How do leaders from the margins cross this geographic and metaphoric distance? Central to the premise of leading from the margins is the belief that there were skills learned in this space— for me, the rural South—that have positively shaped my leadership. Fortunately, I came to realize that my experiences in poverty, those experiences that made me vulnerable, also made me strong.

Taken together, race, gender, class, and rurality combine to not only shape the margins but also to create a deep-seated vulnerability. And, all too often, vulnerability for those in the center is viewed as a weakness, as antithetical to leadership. I actively push back on that notion because I believe that margin-based, mission-driven leadership—to work toward and embrace vocation—in fact demands some degree of vulnerability. To me, vulnerability and courage are twins. To lead courageously is to embrace vulnerability, a vulnerability that often reflects your origins and a courage that was born as part of your story.

For example, as a leader in higher education, you are often called to account not only for your own errors but for systemic issues you inherit on campus and larger issues in the world that reveal themselves on campus. There are times when you are directly responsible—you have made an error in judgment or action—and times when issues are visited upon you. In either case, you must make yourself vulnerable to either say "I am sorry" or simply be present and a witness to the pain being expressed. Both instances require vulnerability and courage. For me, my vulnerability and courage stem not only from my personal demographics but also from how and where I was raised.

Let's take a moment to explore how vulnerability born from class and regional challenges impacts leadership.

Vulnerability

For a long time, I was reluctant to share my story as the daughter of a woman who was born in 1926 in rural North Carolina. As I shared earlier, my mother's birth was unrecorded because of the time and place in which she was born. That is a painful truth that made me feel very vulnerable outside my home community. But what I have come to learn is that, as Brené Brown says, "Vulnerability is the birthplace of innovation, creativity and change." I came to realize that those things that made me vulnerable also made me strong. That it is not at all incompatible to be a good leader and to make yourself vulnerable.

Vulnerability is also important when you think through how you can nurture and unlock leadership in others, which is a key administrative leadership task. For those of us driven by vocation and mission, leadership development may be less about equipping someone with a specific skill set than it is about teaching someone to lead and be courageous and vulnerable. Vulnerability invites learning, collaboration, and an opportunity to lead a community. Courage gives voice to your vulnerability.

I have found that making myself vulnerable and sharing those experiences with others not only strengthens my own leadership ability, but it also encourages others in their desire and ability to lead. For example, I share that I couldn't do the things in college that many are able to take advantage of—play a sport, study abroad, buy a college sweatshirt—because I didn't have the money. I know what it's like to feel like an outsider on a college campus and an interloper when I return home. When I share these vulnerable feelings, I am able to connect with those who are currently having a similar experience and perhaps encourage them to use their challenge to inspire and sustain them as leaders.

As a result, others have begun to share their stories with me. I know of students who were homeless and decided to pursue education to prove their value to their families. I have embraced employees who have had every material need met but who have questioned their value and worth. I have prayed with colleagues who need the love and support of our community to support them through personal crises.

As I think about some of the choices that young people are making today, I think it is because they cannot share their stories of vulnerability and unlock their leadership abilities. In the words of Maya Angelou, "There is no greater agony than bearing an untold story inside you." Wrestling with that story and having that vulnerability locked away can suppress one's leadership ability.

Because I was born in the margins and experienced vulnerability since birth, I know that good leadership is as much about being in relationship as it is about making difficult decisions. For those from the margins, striving to be in relationship with others is inherent in our survival toolkit. Being vulnerable is a way of life that imparts great strength, a strength that can be used to support the humanity, and build the leadership, of another.

I believe that the dearth of strong, diverse leaders today is due, in part, to the fact that leaders from the margins are fearful of being penalized if they share their stories of vulnerability and unlock their leadership abilities. I encourage leaders from the margins to claim and nurture the unique knowledge, the relational and leadership skills the margins hone, and to then deploy that leadership in service of the students we engage with.

What the Margins Frame

Leaders from the margins find ourselves wrestling with cultural notions of what it means to be a leader. Our identities as they relate to race, gender, and economic status often play a dominant fashioning role. However, these are not the only influences on how we understand and carry out our leadership—and perhaps these are not the most pervasive identities for you. You determine what and how the margins in your life drive your leadership.

I have learned from dwelling in the margins that it is important to name these influences and to embrace them as part of your leadership, as opposed to a challenge to your leadership. I have learned that what equipped me on the margins—a sense of connection with those who dwell with me, a desire to help others, a need to give to those who have given me so much—was its own valuable leadership stance. I began to name that which others said would make me vulnerable, that which I knew contained my greatest strength. I encourage you to do the same.

Questions for Reflection

- How does where and how you grew up impact your identity and your leadership?
- As a leader, what are your points of vulnerability that make you strong?
- How can we be vulnerable in order to unlock the leadership potential of another?
- What leadership strengths emerge from the identities and experiences that make you feel vulnerable?

PART II

The Margins Embrace

CHAPTER 6

Leadership Theory from the Margins

So, what does my background have to do with my leadership and, more importantly, what does it have to do with *your* leadership? Allow me to pose a theory of leadership connected to the leadership lessons I learned on the margins, with the hope that it can inform and challenge your own leadership.

For most of us who are working in, or considering leadership in, higher education, it is because we feel a vocational pull toward the development of others. Yet, higher education is not an easy environment within which to lead. The late Peter Drucker is credited with saying that being a college president is one of the four most difficult jobs in the country. This is likely due, in part, to the competing multiple demands of a growing number of constituents, a broken economic model, and the erosion of public trust. With a growing number of colleges closing, birth rates dropping, and derision from all sides of the political spectrum, strong leadership in higher education has likely never been more difficult or more needed. Yet, the average tenure for a college president is slightly less than six years.

According to an Aspen Institute report, today higher education demands courageous leadership in three key areas: maintaining its value as a public good in a time of decreased public trust; balancing high-quality learning experiences with a sustainable financial model, while attending to research, economic development, and national and international concerns within a time of constrained resources; and, most importantly for this book, ensuring "equitable access, opportunity, and success for students of all backgrounds."[1]

To meet all three of the goals outlined in the report, it is essential that higher education leaders at every level place students squarely in the center—and those students and their needs are rapidly changing. Data from the National Center for Education Statistics show that women continue to outpace men in attending college, with 72.5 percent of women high school graduates enrolling in a two- or four-year college, compared to 65.8 percent of men.[2] This disparity between men and women attending college is even greater within low-income communities. Further, while there is a dramatic decline in the number of high school graduates overall, in the United States, any increases in high school student demographics nationally are found among students of color, primarily Latino, Asian, and African-American students.[3] At the same time, the enrollment of lower income students is also increasing. For example, when looking at racial and economic data together, we find that 65 percent of Hispanic and African-American families with college-aged children were below the median US household income of $65,000, likely making a college education feel out of reach financially. Finally, the fastest-growing group of enrolling students are not traditional-aged college students, but adults looking to attain or complete a degree. In order for higher education to continue to thrive, it must be able to serve populations that have historically been underrepresented in the marketplace.

However, the leadership of higher education currently does not reflect those demographics. According to the American Council on Education, in 2017, the profile of the typical college president was a white male, aged sixty, who had been in his position for seven years.[4] Women comprised only 30 percent of college presidents, with leaders of color making up 17 percent of college presidents.

Therefore, the need for leadership, especially the leadership of those from diverse backgrounds—or the margins—is increasingly important. To serve the future students in American higher education, we need a leadership cohort that can not only understand their lived experience, but also leverage that lived experience into strength. A consistent demand from students protesting on college campuses has been the call to diversify the faculty and staff with whom they engage.[5] Often, this call for more diverse leadership has appeared at the very top of lists of student demands, reflecting students' desire and need to see leadership that is reflective of their experience. So how does one begin to think about leadership when hailing from the margins?

The college presidency, like higher education itself, was built around a model, including a leadership profile, that does not resemble me; therefore, wrestling with that became an important part of my leadership journey. Hence, this book was born because I presume there are others who are as impacted by their past as I am—people who attempt to locate themselves in leadership theories but are unable to do so.

The Call to Leadership

With that backdrop in mind, one thing that is clear from the moment you begin to search for a senior-level leadership position is that it is not merely a professional act. A leadership position in higher education demands all of you, twenty-four hours a day, seven days a week. Who you are as a person is as important as your professional competence, and you have to understand yourself to lead others. Because, by definition, leadership demands that there be people you are leading, you must be clear about how you want to lead. Therefore, you may be a leader who likes to be out in front of the crowd, clearing the way for others. Or, perhaps you're a servant leader at the back of the pack, empowering others to blaze their own trail. In either case, leadership requires that you successfully engage with and support others. Leadership is about action, not position. Or, as Margaret Wheatley said, "Leadership is a series of behaviors rather than a role for heroes."[6] So, what, then, does leadership mean for those from the margins?

Many leadership books suggest that leadership skills or the talent needed to be a leader are ingrained—qualities one is born with and only needs to unleash. And, it is likely true that for some, their lived experiences position them to tap into skills they have developed that equip them to lead others. I believe leaders from the margins have those skills, and I explore in this chapter some qualities that those who dwell on the margins develop as part of their lives—qualities that can translate well into strong leadership ability.

In the introduction I indicated that a leader originating from the margins seeks to move across the center space, engage those encountered there, and, of equal importance, reach the other edges of the margin to engage those who have a shared marginal perspective. Leading from the margins demands a dynamic willingness to move through, toward, and within. In my experience, there are two critical strategies that are developed on the margins and that support and guide leaders from the margins: authenticity and mission-driven leadership.

Authenticity

Authenticity is a popular word in the leadership lexicon today. One has only to glance at the thousands of articles readily available to see the importance of being an authentic leader. A recent *Harvard Business Review* article stated, "Withholding your true self puts a cap on trust and on your ability to lead."[7] Bringing one's wholehearted, authentic self to the workplace engenders support, empowerment, and a shared commitment to leadership.

The *Harvard Business Review* study of successful African-American women graduates also makes two essential points related to authenticity. First, they identified that "the women [they] studied developed three skills that were key to their resilience: emotional intelligence, authenticity, and agility." They go on to indicate that, for Black women, the need for an authentic voice to support leadership is complicated by both their sex and their race: "A woman's sense of authenticity—a conviction that her outward behavior is consistent with her inner values and identity—is essential to her emotional well-being, productivity, and personal satisfaction. Yet because black women are under pressure to conform to white workplace norms, even highly successful black women, such as graduates of Harvard Business School, report they find it difficult 'to be themselves' at work.

Thus, black women pursuing careers in gendered workplaces are continually walking a tightrope between 'fitting in' and feeling authentic."[8]

Similarly, Charisse Jones and Kumea Shorter-Gooden explore Black women's struggles with authenticity in the professional world at great length and find that in an effort to support and comfort others, Black women must often suppress and silence their own authentic needs. The authors write:

> Our research shows that in response to their relentless oppression, Black women in our country have had to perfect what we call "shifting," a sort of subterfuge that African Americans have long practiced to ensure their survival in our society. . . . Black women are relentlessly pushed to serve and satisfy others and made to hide their true selves. . . . From one moment to the next, they change their outward behavior, attitude, or tone. . . . And shifting has become such an integral part of Black women's behavior that some adopt an alternate pose or voice as easily as they blink their eyes or draw breath—without thinking, and without realizing that the emptiness they feel and the roles they must play may be directly related.[9]

To lead effectively, to know oneself, to engender the trust of others, to be disciplined in the pursuit of one's personal and institutional mission, a leader cannot be left empty. Leaders must have a wellspring of courage and ideas from which to draw and cannot sacrifice that for the sake of others. To successfully navigate and persevere as a leader, you must also be willing to embrace and express those identities, and the challenges and opportunities attendant to those identities.

While many may think that just showing up "as you are" is what it means to be authentic, genuine authenticity demands much more. There seems to be consensus that authentic leaders spend time exploring their own identities, strengths, and weaknesses and know themselves well; are willing to share and build trust with everyone they work with; are disciplined in their pursuits; are reliable, trustworthy colleagues; seek and accept feedback; and are committed to a personal mission to achieve success for their organizations and themselves.[10] At its core, authentic leadership comes from knowing our many identities and deploying those identities in pursuit of our mission. While perhaps an overused phrase, authentic leadership is about expressing your truth. But, it's important to first do the interior work of exploring, acknowledging, interrogating, and reflecting on that truth before espousing it. Authentic leadership is about recognizing that who you are is not static as a leader; that, in fact, we authentically change as we have new experiences and navigate new challenges. Authentic leadership is embracing who you are while at the same time allowing who you are to respond to what is happening around you. Authentic leadership is not something you put on and take off like an item of clothing. It's not something you can appropriate because it is who you think you should be to meet the world's definition. Authentic leadership iterates from your core and slowly evolves in response to your experiences.

As you know, my authentic identity is as a Southern woman, an African American, a member of Generation X, someone who comes from a lower socioeconomic status, and someone who spent much of my life in predominantly white institutions. Each of these demographic markers serves as my foundation but they have evolved in response to my lived experience.

Because of my willingness to be authentic in my leadership and share my story as a leader, students began to share their stories and authentic identities with me. The same is true for faculty and administrative colleagues who have chosen to share their hearts with me because I was willing to authentically share mine with them.

These moments of connection are what enables effective leaders. Successful leadership, while demanding content expertise, is rarely determined by an ability to master a spreadsheet, budget, or other tactical skills. Successful leadership hinges upon your ability to be in deep relationship with those you are leading. To create those relationships, inspire and engage others, be disciplined in your pursuits on behalf of your organization, and fulfill your mission, you must embrace your authentic voice.

Of course, many structures and policies need to change to better support leaders from the margins. Some of those realities we can control by asserting and enforcing our rights in the workplace and equipping ourselves with the skills needed to succeed. Some of those structures require a collective effort to right, such as by fighting for pay equity or paid family leave, and it is critical to acknowledge and seek to address those structures.

That said, it is also critically important to focus on our internal authentic leadership capacity. At the end of the day, no structural changes—no amount of support, no number of networking events, no advanced degrees—will work unless you believe in and are able to reveal your authentic self. Too often, our most dangerous messages come from within as we suppress who and what we are in an effort to please others. Instead, we must believe in our value and authentic voice, in our worthiness, if we are going to embrace who we are as leaders. Because who we are is— simply put—enough. Once you trust that authentic voice and have that clarity, your life's mission, purpose, calling, and vocation can emerge, and another critical leadership criteria for those in the margins comes forth: mission-driven leadership. Honoring your authentic self and voice then enables you to clearly define your authentic leadership mission—a mission that began in the margins.

Mission-Driven Leadership

The questions that I wrestled with throughout my career as I balanced my marginality and my professional life may sound familiar to you: What is it that compelled me forward when the journey didn't always make sense? When I had no rational reason to believe I could be a leader? You see, the world consistently told me that I'm not a leader, I don't look like a leader, there aren't many leaders like me. How much of that had I internalized? What made me decide to become vulnerable to challenges of leadership and what gives me courage now as I lead an organization committed to developing the leadership skills of others? To be clear, good discernment may take you to an unexpected outcome, but you've been answering these questions for a long time.

I began to realize that in my life, as is likely the case in your life, there has long been a mission that I have found myself on, a vocational call I have been responding to. To be clear, I'm talking about the mission of your heart, the vocation of your spirit. Your purpose and your calling. As leaders, we so often think of institutional mission. But I don't mean that one. I mean the mission that tethers your lived experiences and your heart. A mission that at times I was initially unaware of and, at other times, I consciously refused to recognize.

I do have a personal and professional mission that has led me through my life and career. I know that you have a vocational and personal mission call, too. I call this mission-driven leadership. This is so critically important when you are from the margins and navigating a world that may not always support you or your mission. Sometimes you must sustain yourself. As you read, I invite you to begin to think about your mission and how it aligns, or does not align, with your professional aspirations.

The presence of a mission enables leaders to sustain themselves, and it prepares their organizations and communities to succeed in the face of daunting odds and challenges. In the words of Parker Palmer, "Before I can tell my life what I want to do with it, I must listen to my life telling me who I am."[11]

As I shared in chapter one, my mission began in Kittrell, North Carolina. I certainly grew up in a home filled with love, but that was our most abundant—and at times only—resource. Yet, our focus as a family was never on what we lacked. Rather, my mother intentionally focused us on the idea that we had much more than other people. And, while that argument could not be made regarding material possessions, she always said that because you have a functioning brain, you have more than, and an obligation to give back to, others. I can recall this statement being made when we were at home, being dropped off for school, even in the grocery store. It always came back to the fact that you aren't defined by what material objects you have but by what your intellectual resources are, and—of equal, maybe even greater importance—how you utilize those resources in support of another. I learned early on that everything that sustains me is within me. My mission was born with an eye toward service and an abundance mindset.

I share this beginning because a mission is what will sustain you in the challenges you will face as a leader. It's what enables you to engage with the tyranny of the to-do list but not be defined by it or other external factors. For example, because of my early lessons and my mission, I cannot view the world through a lens of what is lacking. Also, I do not base what I (or my institution) have and what I have to contribute in comparison to what others have. While benchmarking is important when measuring quantitative progress, I am steadfast in my position that I only compete against myself, that life is not a zero-sum game, and that, in fact, spending your time comparing yourself or your institution to others will either leave you with a tremendous inferiority complex or make you terribly arrogant. Neither of those positions will support an authentic leader.

My experiences growing up also make me somewhat unafraid. You will encounter people who will go above and beyond to bring you down simply because of who you are. You must know who you are and what you are about. You must be authentic not just to be a good leader but also to be yourself and nurture the resilience needed to lead.

My mission is to create and support educational equity and opportunity. Yet my work as an administrator includes responding to emails, attending too many meetings, high levels of accountability, and other daily tasks, but those are the things that enable my vocation. My vocation and mission are defined by my work toward equity. My daily administrative tasks are what enable me to fulfill that mission. As you think about your vocation and leadership, are you able to separate the vocation from the tasks? That's essential, as they are not the same.

Today, amid one of the most challenging times in higher education, economically, demographically, and in terms of public perception, because of my mission and sense of abundance, I know that I am privileged to have what I have and that my obligation to serve others is not waning. I know that, together, we must face these challenges head-on in order to be able to benefit another and support all in the margins.

An Unwavering Will

My mission was conceived through challenges and, like many in the margins, has been nurtured by courage and resolve. But things are not that straightforward. Like many of you, I wrestled with my mission. I didn't want to do the difficult things. I wanted to retreat into vulnerability as opposed to leveraging it. You see, as I became an adult from the margins and a world of opportunities in the center made themselves available, I began to think that I could be driven by other things aside from my mission—by my desire for earnings, a grand title, etc. Some of you have been equally driven by the center and I could argue that perhaps that is a rite of passage. There were moments when I wanted to reject my mission and the margins and focus on me and my desires; to think not about what obligation I had to the world, but to only focus on my own vested self-interest. I wanted to forget about what my mother taught me. Ironically, it is most often in the face of opportunity that these tendencies arise: A headhunter calls or we get an unearned promotion. It is in the face of great opportunity that we can begin to believe the press releases about ourselves—I am as great as that newspaper says I am. But I would caution us that mission-driven leadership has to approach opportunity differently.

First, we must discern which opportunities promote our mission and which promote ourselves. How do we live our vocation as opposed to contorting who we are in order to carry out the mission of another? How do we fashion our own desires and outcomes in a world that wants to tell you who you should be and limits you accordingly?

Next, I have also learned that humility plays a role in how we engage opportunities. We know that great leaders have a vision for the future, the skills to implement that vision, and the humility to share that success with others. In fact, when Harvard Business School researched the best leaders of our time, they found that they had a compelling and rare mix of a strong will to achieve success and an equally strong desire to exert humility when sharing that success. This balance is called Level Five Leadership and is incredibly difficult to achieve.[12] At the same time, we are too often quick to self-deprecate when success is at hand. I have often spoken about the challenge of lack of confidence in terms of being leaders—and there is great risk and disservice in that—but there is also some power in the ability to be humble. The challenge is to manage and leverage both. Have the confidence to own your success and the humility to share credit for that success with others. Having the confidence to take the risk of applying for that stretch position is, in part, born from having the humility to listen to others who encourage you to do so. Humility is often thought of as demureness. But humility is also trusting people who say they see something in you and listening to them.

Even with a Level Five Leadership perspective, success opportunities that promote our mission are often difficult, slow, and nonlinear. We must step out on faith—whatever that means and feels like for you. We have to believe in the value of our personal mission so that we stay with it. We must learn that technical skill and success are not sufficient. That our mission demands a level of selflessness, humility, and resolve that are difficult to balance, and yet it is essential that they co-occur.

Humility means, in the face of numerous and compelling opportunities, checking in with your mission and asking if this opportunity is bigger than you. Is it worthy of your mission? And then, committing the resources to completing the task with an unwavering will. So, I ask you to consider: How can you launch your leadership in ways that enable you to bring both humility and unrelenting will to the forefront?

Leadership across Time and Place

The poet Rumi wrote, "If you are here unfaithfully with us, you are causing terrible damage."[13] I come back to this quote often because I think it truly relates to authentic leadership development. For me, being connected to the time and place where one leads is incredibly important. By connected, I mean invested in the time, the heritage, and the location. This takes on special meaning in certain sectors in higher education like women's colleges, Catholic higher education, and historically Black colleges and universities. Today, my work tethers me in southwestern Virginia. I have the good fortune of being able to travel widely while representing Hollins University. Yet, I can never forget that representing Hollins University, by definition, means representing the history and legacy of a community and what it stands for.

Leaders that are new within a community are often eager to make changes to better the place in which they find themselves. Often, changes need to be made to ensure an institution, a business, a community continue to function well. But, as a leader, if I am here only to critique and change the community, or to remake the community in my own image, then I am doing terrible damage. A mission-driven leader seeks to illuminate a community by connecting with it.

Similarly, a mission-driven leader must be faithful to the time in which they are serving. I can neither pine for what used to be nor stand and wait for what may come. A mission-driven leader must be immersed in the present, using the past to educate oneself about current circumstances and visioning how to illuminate the future, but squarely planted in the present. You are currently on your mission. It is not something that you will do tomorrow. It is the life you are living today. Your future is not something we await. It is something we create. In the words of John Schaar: "The future is not a result of choices among alternative paths offered by the present, but a place that is created—created first in mind and will, created next in activity. The future is not some place we are going to, but one we are creating. The paths are not to be found, but made, and the activity of making them changes both the maker and the destination."[14]

Mission-driven leadership is about creating that path. For leaders from the margins, the question is: How do you create this path while using your unique strengths to reach out to others on the margins in order to equip them to be strong leaders as well? How is your leadership illuminating a path to the future for all?

For example, in 2021, I had the privilege of leading the team that created the Hollins Opportunity for Promise through Education (HOPE) scholarship program. Simply stated, HOPE allows young women from within a forty-mile radius who have family incomes of less than $50,000 to attend Hollins for four years tuition-free. Being a part of creating this program was one of the most impactful moments in my life. You see, it allowed me to address my own desire to create educational equity. However, it also magnified the importance of the local community on leadership. Hollins was founded in Hollins (Roanoke), Virginia over

180 years ago. Throughout much of its history it was viewed as a place of wealth and privilege, separate and apart from much of what happened in Roanoke. However, to be an authentic leader in this time and place, I strongly felt the need to connect with and support the Roanoke community. It is what I am called to do and it was critical as someone from the margins to use my platform and resources to support others in the margins, including the communities of which they are a part. This alignment between personal mission, which is developed through one's marginality, institutional mission, and local community, provides a wholeness that reinforces one's authenticity.

What the Margins Frame

Authenticity and mission-driven leadership, taken together, allow you to leverage critical skills born on the margins: intentionality and leadership in relationship.

Intentionality. To be able to emerge from the margins, in any pursuit, demands a great degree of intentionality. While some are able to rely on family wealth, pedigree, or a strong network to pave a way forward, those who exist on the margins rarely have such a support system. Even with great support from one's family, the professional opportunities to be successful do not readily present themselves to those on the margins. This intentionality is evident as early as high school, and perhaps even earlier.

Recall my story about my encounter with a guidance counselor in tenth grade. Intentionality was essential in even pursuing the idea of college, as there certainly would not have been outreach from her to me as there would have been for my more center-oriented peers. I knew that my future was largely in my own hands and demanded intentional action. The purpose was clear: to create a new and different life for myself.

These skills, born on the margins, are incredibly important in leadership. Currently, it is popular for strong leadership to look effortless or casual. Bill Gates, the late Steve Jobs, Mark Zuckerberg, and other tech giants transmit this notion of casual leadership through their appearance and the pervasive story that successful leadership can begin by toying around in a garage—a boy and his dream. Yet, when examined closely, each of these successful leaders was intentional and purposeful in their pursuits.

Leadership in relationship. "If I'm the smartest person in the room, I'm in the wrong room." One of my vice presidents was known for this saying, which I found incredibly thoughtful and discerning. So often the notion is that good leadership is about being, and actively displaying that you are, the smartest person in the room. For many on the margins, or even those who wrestle with imposter syndrome, the pressure of being the smartest in the room, combined with being in the center of the room, can feel overwhelming and off-putting. This notion is a bigger trap in higher education than anywhere else, perhaps. We are in the "smart" business. We use intelligence as a kind of coin of the realm. But we must decide: Are we in the business of proclaiming our own smarts, or cultivating the growth of intellectual potential among our students? If it is the latter, then we have to be vulnerable to the inevitability that we will encounter others who are smarter than we are—in fact, our job is to make certain that we do.

Yet, perhaps the single biggest leadership lesson I have learned is that the leader is not, and should not strive to be, the smartest person in the room. A good leader seeks to hire people smarter than they are—people they can learn from. Automatically, that means that the leader is surrounded by incredibly smart people.

At the same time, the leader is unique in the rooms in which they dwell. The leader has the unique obligation—I would even be so forceful as to say the unique demand—to be in active, generative relationship with every person with whom they share time and space. The most clarifying moment on my leadership journey was when I realized that being a leader means being in relationship with every person you lead even when, especially when, you may not want to be. This realization relieved much of the pressure I had experienced that was compromising my leadership. While I must make difficult decisions, draft ambitious plans, and meet a variety of metrics, recognizing that I lead in relationship makes each of those tasks easier. Additionally, leading in relationship develops the trust needed to make and withstand those decisions.

These hard-won skills are nurtured on the margins. In the margins, you learn how to engage and support those in the margins with you, and the world tells you that "real success" means making it to the center. As a result, leaders from the margins have learned—of necessity—to be in relationship with a variety of people and ideas.

Being a Catalyst

As accomplished leaders, there are questions we are used to being asked: What do you do? What do you plan to do next? How do you do it all?

Recently I was asked if I envision myself being a college president for a long time. Do I like being a college president? This was a relatively straightforward question, and I immediately knew the right answer. The right answer is yes. You achieve bonus points if you articulate why you say yes: I love the people with whom I work, it's an incredible opportunity to have an impact on a community, I get to be around students all day. So as this question was asked, the answer was abundantly clear: just say yes and deliver the spiel that you've rehearsed and they expect.

But I didn't say yes. I broke the script. I made it impossible for that person to not listen to me. You see, part of the reason we don't listen today is because we presume we already know what the other person is going to say. Even if we've only recently met, we have scripts in our mind that we expect others to play out. Leaders have a script to follow—a script that was written in the center, not the margins.

But I no longer want to fulfill the script. I want to share my truth and, even more, I want to hear others' truths. So, when hailing from the margins, we must put aside our scripts, our expectations, and our demands for how others respond to us.

So, do I think I'll be a college president for a long time? In some ways, the answer doesn't matter. My fancy, impressive role doesn't matter. It's not the position or title that moves me. What I want is not to be a president per se but to be a person who catalyzes young women's ability to find their voice. Someone who does this with an eye toward equity, a heart filled with hope and courage, and a willingness to model being vulnerable. Why? Because for a young woman to find, nurture, and trust her voice—to become the leader we want her to be—she must have a mind to do each of those things.

My job as president is to create a college community wherein every student, beginning on that first day, feels at home. Feels valued. Feels strength and promise in her future. It is for that purpose that I am willing to stretch, risk, and be vulnerable. To move in spaces where I feel "other." So long as colleges need someone to catalyze the lives of young women, then I will be that person. A catalyst. I will do it proudly with the title "president," but you and I know that's my title, not my mission or my work.

Questions for Reflection

As you think about who you are, the complexity of your identities, and the authentic voice you want to bring to leadership, please ask yourself the following:

- What is your authentic leadership voice?
- How do your intersecting marginal identities inform that voice?
- What opportunities are ahead of you that are worthy of your mission? How will you pursue them by leading with the inherent strengths you bring from the margins?
- How do you share and live your authentic identities and voice in ways that enhance your leadership, within a world that may not fully understand or value those multiple and overlapping identities?
- How are you connected to a time and place in your organization and how do you use your position to enhance that connection, especially with others in the margins?
- What catalytic actions are you engaging in? What is your current catalyzing agenda?
- How is your leadership illuminating the community and illuminating a path to the future?

Answering these questions is an essential first step in revealing and leveraging your essential leadership voice.

CHAPTER 7

The Vocational Cycle to Support Institutional Justice

Now that we have a vision of how we can navigate our own leadership callings, let's return to reflecting on how our identities can impact our work as leaders. Many leaders from the margins feel called to transform institutions to better serve others. Previously cited articles by McCallum and Waring both speak to the unique opportunities and challenges African Americans face in their leadership, as many find they are leading not only for their own—or even their institutions'—benefit but to make the world better.[1]

For leaders from the margins, this desire to transform often bumps up against strong institutional cultural norms that must be navigated for the sake of the leader, those served, and the institutions. This work often reveals itself in a desire to create more equitable spaces. This chapter seeks to address how leaders

This chapter is adapted from Mary Dana Hinton, "The Vocational Cycle to Support Institutional Justice: A Pathway for Scholars of Color to Transform Institutional Life and Governance," in *Teaching for a Culturally Diverse and Racially Just World*, ed. Eleazar S. Fernandez, 184–201 (Eugene, OR: Cascade Books, 2013). Used with permission of Wipf and Stock Publishers, www.wipfandstock.com.

from the margins, especially leaders of color, in higher education engage institutional life and governance to create and sustain just institutional cultures.

It is important to note that other marginalized leaders face similar concerns. Women and LGBTQ+ scholars and leaders are caught in this same dynamic for many of the same reasons. If an LGBTQ+ leader wants to advocate for greater inclusivity—a broad rethinking of academic subjects/curricular topics to include gay, trans, and nonbinary writers, a reconceptualization of residential housing practices to carve out safe and comfortable options for LGBTQ+ students, etc.—his/her/their commitment to this work can come into conflict with alumni, boards, and/or public perceptions and biases. If a woman in a key position of leadership wants to advocate for greater equity in, for example, the allocation of funding across athletic programs to create greater opportunities for women to compete at the highest level, she might encounter deep disagreement among older alumni who view this as overly "woke" or misguided. It is essential to have a process to support navigating these landscapes to accomplish this important and authentic work.

While I am engaging this topic at the institutional level, my central thesis is that when electing to serve an institution and committing to creating a more just institution, one must discern, be faithful to, and promote personal vocational aspirations and allow them to drive the daily work that shapes the institution. It is important to note here my intentional use of the word vocation. Critical to the discussion of leading from the margins is understanding how personal vocation—which emerges from identity—can be leveraged as an agent of change, moving institutions of higher education toward greater racial justice. Vocation certainly connotes "work" or even "career," but it also speaks to something deeper—something that compels your effort well beyond the daily work rewards of salary, title, and other incentives. Vocation is what tethers your heart to the work and, ideally, the institution. Because vocation demands more than work, it also leaves you more vulnerable to the happenings and culture of the workplace. It also demands that you be courageous in your response. However, if you are willing to be vulnerable and courageous in service to your institution, change is possible.

I describe the notion of using vocation to shape an institution, and allowing the institution to shape vocation, as a Vocational Cycle to Support Institutional Justice. This cycle was developed in response to my analyses of my experiences in higher education as a person from the margins. It is only by understanding and acting upon this cycle between the institution and the individual that institutional justice supporting the margins can be achieved. I will discuss each aspect of the cycle shortly; a graphic depiction to keep in mind is shown in figure 1.

Figure 1. The Vocational Cycle to Support Institutional Justice

Personal Context and Institutional Climate

How one understands, engages, responds to, and shapes institutional life and governance is quite heavily shaped by personal context. I've spent a great deal of time in the earlier chapters of this book describing my personal context and situating myself within higher education. The experiences that I bring with me not only fashion how I interpret my personal experience in higher education, but they are the lens through which I understand and interpret the institutions of which I have been, and continue to be, a part.

While I believe my experiences to be typical of what many people from the margins face in the academy, I do not claim that my experiences are either universal or exclusively unique. Rather, my institutional experiences have been influenced by my context. Thus, the offerings of this chapter must be situated and understood within that context.

Similarly, my experiences do not represent the totality of the types of experiences possible in higher education. However, the consistency of my experiences in terms of the situations I have observed, and how individuals have responded to me as a Black woman, is notable. Further, that consistency is reflected regardless of the role occupied in higher education: student, faculty, student affairs staff member, or senior administrator. Given the consistency across institution type and the consistency across roles, it is legitimate to draw some conclusions about institutional climate in higher education.

I believe that higher education has significant room for growth to support the success of people from the margins. With that backdrop in mind, what are the experiences of people of color in higher education? Or, what is the institutional climate within which students, faculty, and administrators of color dwell? Whether as a student, faculty member, staff or senior administrator, my experience was often one of balancing competing forces. As discussed earlier, I have found that, as a Black woman, I was faced with dialectics that required careful negotiation to be successful. Three specific dialectics will now be explored: unrealistic power vs. powerlessness, underutilization/low expectations vs. being overworked, and engaging authentically vs. hiding the authentic self to attain and maintain a place at the leadership table. These dialectics are likely common among those who hail from the margins.

Negotiating Dialectics in Higher Education

The first dynamic, unrealistic power vs. powerlessness, takes different forms depending on one's position in higher education, though it is active regardless of role and status. At times, institutions ascribe great power to people of color or women. The power is not, however, the type that can facilitate change. Rather, the person becomes the universal representative of their demographic. For example, regardless of my role, whether as a student or a senior administrator, there were moments when I represented to those in the room the totality of their experience with Black women. I held the power to define their image of Black women and how they would respond to Black women in the future. I became the universal Black woman, and my words were viewed as representing all Black women or, at times, all Black people; an individual whose words and actions carried unrealistic, albeit heady, authority. There is, on the surface, great power in this dynamic. Diana Hayes notes that Black women in academia "have been marginalized, yet, at the same time, strangely empowered, given authority we have not sought to speak for all Black women and, indeed, all Blacks."[2]

However, the power quickly becomes burdensome and morphs into feelings of powerlessness as one recognizes that they are not heard for their unique opinion or ability to facilitate change, but only in terms of how well they align with perceived notions of their demographic. In contrast to feeling powerful, the opposing dialectic occurs when people ascribe to you the characteristics that *they* want, based on their prior experiences with Black women, and you are powerless to shape those perceptions. At its worst, you are shaped and perceived by negative prior experiences: any misdeed caused by any Black woman at any time can make those around you perceive you suspiciously. Being unable to define oneself is the very definition of being powerless.

The burden of this dynamic is particularly acute. At times, the power of representing an entire demographic is overwhelming and fashions one's behaviors and responses beyond the realm of authenticity, a dangerous position that will be discussed in detail later. Equally burdensome is the lack of power, and the subjection to someone's delayed response to experiences that they had with folks of similar demographics previously. Therefore, the initial dynamic, one that was uniformly experienced at each level of higher education, regardless of role, is an often repeated dynamic and the one most likely to resonate with other scholars of color.

The second dynamic that has been noted among those from the margins is that of underutilization vs. being overworked. As discussed earlier, it is well understood that women and minorities often feel the need to outperform their colleagues in order to achieve even modest recognition. As such, there may be an assumption that key concepts and tasks will elude them. Whether this experience happens at the student or senior administrator level, the belief is that because of your demographic, you cannot be given leadership tasks. The other side of this dialectic is a powerful desire to overperform to prove one's ability. This overperformance is generally not limited to high-level tasks, but often happens with tasks of varying levels of importance, resulting in the student, faculty, and administrator of color risking burnout because of taking on excessive amounts of work to prove their value. Of course, the argument can be made that all new employees work extra hard to demonstrate their value. While true, the initial power dialectic heightens, and extends, the need for people of color to prove themselves, thus leading to and emboldening this dynamic.

Patitu and Hinton suggest that faculty of color, in particular, have powerful narratives surrounding this dynamic.[3] They reported faculty descriptions of feeling isolated, being subjected to different standards, having feelings of being "watched," and having to repeatedly demonstrate their value, especially as they were on the tenure track. Further, the secretive nature of the tenure and promotion process exacerbated the need to overachieve to receive professional recognition. Underutilization vs. overwork, like unrealistic power vs. powerlessness, has as much to do with those surrounding the leader of color as it does with the scholar themselves. The dialectic is triggered by the reaction of those surrounding the leader. They then must determine how they want to react to the dynamic and how they will resolve the resulting tension.

In no dialectic is the leader's reaction more important than in the last one, which leads directly to the Vocational Cycle to

Support Institutional Change. The final dynamic is that wherein one has to balance being one's authentic self and advocating as needed versus maintaining a place at the leadership table, at times by hiding one's authentic self.

While the power dynamic and the utilization dynamic are consistent across roles, the authenticity dynamic is much more acute as one rises through the ranks of higher education. In part, this is due to an increased level of access to the decision-making structure of the college. As that level of access increases, one must be more intentional in deciding which issues, in the universe of issues, to explore and advocate for and against, and the dynamic becomes more critical. Further, as real power, not the perceived power discussed in the first dynamic, increases, this dynamic becomes increasingly fraught.

In response, some scholars and administrators of color in the academy may choose to suppress and silence their own authentic needs (Charisse Jones and Kumea Shorter-Gooden's notion of "shifting"[4]), and others may choose to disengage at critical times as a means of self-protection. Evans and Herr suggest African-American women, who are subject to both racial and gender discrimination, may well materially disengage from their professional lives as a survival strategy: "In order to avoid a negative situation, a person may decline to participate in a particular activity, modify life-styles, or redirect ambitions and goals. It seems reasonable to assume that African American women, who perceive themselves as victims of double discrimination and prejudice, might use some of these techniques in their attempt to avoid the probable thwarting of their aspirations in the labor market."[5]

Everyone, no matter their identities, must at times determine when to speak up and when to maintain silence. However, this dynamic may be more consequential for scholars and administrators of color given the dialectics discussed earlier. At the highest levels of academic administration, decisions have wider-reaching impact and may provide the best opportunity for improving campus climate. Leaders of color must determine how much of their authentic selves to reveal to support change. With increased authority, power, and importance, the obligation to carefully negotiate this dynamic is vital.

How one resolves this dialectic, or any of the dialectics, is not proscribed. Instead, one must be awake to, and aware of, the dynamics at play. To successfully challenge institutional culture, one must name the dynamics, help others to see and acknowledge them, dwell in the tension of how to resolve the dialectic, and then go about authentically addressing and learning from the dynamic. Most importantly, the need to negotiate the final dialectic sets forth the rationale for the Vocational Cycle.

Vocational Cycle to Support Institutional Justice

By employing the Vocational Cycle to Support Institutional Justice, those from the margins can move beyond the expectations and demands of the center and use their efforts to support and bring forth institutional justice. This cycle was created based on my personal context coming from the margins, experience with the dialectics, and attempts to engage in institutional transformation.

Personal context and understanding. As established earlier, personal context and understanding are powerful, shaping forces. Not only do they fashion how one experiences the world around them, but personal context and understanding also shape how one responds to the world and impacts it. In higher education, the context is shaped by experiences as a student and continues to be shaped as one progresses through higher education professional culture.

As discussed in part I of this book, it is clear that being in the margins forces leaders to develop a number of strategies, internally and externally, which enable them to address the challenges they face and continue to move forward, both professionally and personally. For example, Moore's qualitative research found that women often live out their professional lives utilizing and capitalizing on the following qualities: facing unexpected turns, trusting spiritual-intuitive knowing, analyzing and responding to social contexts, standing for justice, committing to make a difference, helping others be who they can be, building bridges, practicing hospitality, valuing women's communities, caring for self, and practicing humor.[6] Given the diversity of Moore's sample, it is reasonable to assume its applicability to women of a variety of demographics.

Vocation. Clearly, context frames vocation. For many, vocation is not merely a clear career path. Rather, it is viewed as a mission or divine fashioning of one's energies. Clarity about vocation is achieved through a process of discernment, wherein one must align their context, experiences, and potential.

Surely the commonalities of personal context provide some insight into vocation for people from the margins. Moore, Patitu and Hinton, and others have articulated the many common factors that women employ as they approach and engage their vocation.[7] For African-American women, race and gender are also undoubtedly active forces shaping vocation.

The premise of the cycle is that institutional justice is impacted by, and impacts, the vocation of the leader from the margin. Black women and others from the margins seeking to shape a just institutional life and climate will acknowledge their vocational call in support of institutional justice and make occupational choices directly aligned with this vocation.

Occupational choices within an institution. If authentically living into vocation, one's occupational choices—both immediate and long-term—will maximize personal context and vocational choices and capitalize on them. To be successful in supporting institutional transformation, these choices must be driven by the desire to serve an institution fully and in ways that allow vocation to positively transform the institution. There is a deep tension associated with *serving* an institution and *transforming it* in pursuit of a vocation or mission-driven calling. Of course, at a deep level, any institution that rolls on without a serious conversation about equity and inclusion will not survive and thrive. To serve the institution *we must transform it.* However, interested parties with deep ties to the institution may not be ready to embrace those transformative changes.

Therefore, to make choices that are not in alignment with vocation is to do both professional and personal damage. When occupational choices, whether daily decisions or long-range occupational planning, run afoul of vocational choices, one is, in many ways, denying personal context and the individual becomes divided. Parker Palmer notes that we live a divided life when choices are made that are not in alignment: "I pay a steep price when I live a divided life, feeling fraudulent, anxious about being found out, depressed by the fact that I am denying my own selfhood. . . . How can I affirm another's integrity when I defy my own? A fault line runs down the middle of my life, and whenever it cracks open—divorcing my words and actions from the truth I hold within—things around me get shaky and start to fall apart."[8] Undoubtedly, the dynamic Palmer articulates is heightened for people from the margins in higher education, as the dialectics discussed previously increase susceptibility to feeling anxious and on shaky ground. If occupational choices to resolve the dialectics and to enable true vocation to shine through are not made, then the fault lines Palmer describes can surely engulf leaders of color. Therefore, it is imperative that the occupational choices leaders make serve their own vocational needs to truly serve the institution and move it toward justice.

As an example, recall that many minorities enter administrative roles citing the ability to give back to their communities as important. This might well be attributed to the fact that there is a belief that institutional change can happen more readily at the institutional or administrative level than at the classroom level. This is not to argue the veracity of that belief, but rather to acknowledge that perhaps many professionals of color elect the administrative route because it enables them to live into their vocation. Similarly, those who remain in the classroom, squarely focused on the personal development of their students, may be doing so in order to live deeply into their vocation and transform institutions in that way. In either instance, faculty and administrators of color are making occupational choices that support their vocation and have the potential to shape and transform institutions.

Institutional life and governance. As indicated earlier, personal context, especially for African-American women, often includes mothering, bridge building, humor, mentoring, caring for, and nurturing others and self, drawing on history and a commitment to improving the future for others. Therefore, how these strategies are carried out in occupational choices and behaviors will drive how one engages institutional life and governance. These strategies, often dismissed as soft, are the very characteristics needed to drive and support institutional justice. It is only by actively employing these strategies that institutional life and governance are influenced.

While the institution is the level of discussion, higher education institutions are merely a collective of people, seemingly working together toward the same mission. If a person from the margins is going to move their institution toward greater racial justice, it is only by approaching each person, task, and challenge with their most authentic selves and by employing these strategies that transformation will take place. We must bring our full vocational aspirations not only to the occupational choices we make but also to the ways we dwell within our institutions and engage governance. Palmer writes, "In fact, when we live by the soul's imperatives, we gain the courage to serve institutions more faithfully, to help them resist their tendency to default on their own missions."[9] The missions of most colleges and universities speak, explicitly or implicitly, to the role of education in creating a more just society. It is the collective of people within the institution who are charged with carrying out that mission. This can only be done when our interactions in institutional life and governance structures are driven, first and foremost, by our ability to authentically relate to one another and remain focused on mission. Institutional mothering means that we explore the governance and institutional structures that have historically sustained institutions, but we do so with a critical eye that enables us to reshape those structures so that they are more just and supportive of future generations, regardless of demographics.

Institutional climate. If one is authentically engaging institutional life and governance using vocation, and *de facto* one's personal context, then the institutional climate will undoubtedly shift. Institutional climate is the primary point of impact in terms of transforming our institutions. Therefore, all that we bring to bear in our personal context and vocational discernment has the power to shape the climate. Our vocational choices inform how we engage the governance structures and how we address justice across the campus as opposed to in our own siloed areas. We are open about our desire to have a unified, as opposed to divided, experience on campus and to seek ways to allow others to have the same. When we enable our personal context to shape the institutional climate, when we "rejoin soul and role," it becomes challenging for institutions to perpetuate injustice. The challenges cannot be ignored and change left as something hoped for. Rather, we embrace what brought us to this point, both positive and negative, and use that to change the climate.

Let me be very clear: It is not easy to do this, and the headwinds you face will be strong. In fact, as an institution begins to change, the winds may increase before they shift in the direction you need them. I believe that these hard moments are inflection points for many leaders from the margins. Because you have made yourself vulnerable and courageously committed to change, you may well become a target. Therefore, in order to truly live into this cycle, you have to make certain that the institution is worthy of this level of commitment and is truly aligned with your vocation. You will be giving fully of yourself, and you want to make certain that you have the hope and legitimate prospect for institutional change.

A return to personal context and understanding. The shift in campus climate, then, immediately circles back to impact personal context and understanding, thus bringing us back to the beginning of the cycle. A changed institution has new needs and new opportunities for progress and transformation. The institution shifts the context within which we dwell. As agents of change, we then need to determine how best to re-engage the institution to continuously facilitate change. It is when the institution is allowed to impact our context that we can review and re-engage our own vocation, providing us with the skills and temerity needed to make the necessary occupational choices to impact institutional transformation. Michael Jinkins, writing about teaching and writing and their relationship, articulates the importance of willingness to being shaped by external forces:

> The courage to make oneself vulnerable is the common point for the vocations of teaching and writing. When we say that good teaching and good writing call us beyond ourselves into relationships that can transform us in ways we never imagined, we must also confess that the changes we face may inspire dread as much as joy. If we are unwilling to risk transformation at the hands of our students and colleagues, our readers, editors, and reviewers, we are unlikely to enjoy either of these vocations very much. However, if we can deliver ourselves into the hands of others, and learn to respect not only the others, but the disciplines and the risks our vocations entail, perhaps we can become good teachers and good writers, and maybe even good people.[10]

While Jinkins specifically references teaching and writing, the work toward institutional justice equally demands being vulnerable to critique and influence in order to develop an evolving authentic voice. The Vocational Cycle to Support Institutional Justice requires constantly exploring and engaging our context so that we are energized to do the work of institutional transformation. The cycle, like our institutions, should never be satisfied. We must constantly explore, and re-explore, personally and institutionally, what we are called to do (our vocation) and be prepared to indicate if we are fully living into that vocation and, if so, are living it justly. There is ample opportunity for you to discern that, in fact, an institution is not aligned with your vocation. While we must all "bear our share," you must be clear-eyed about the alignment between your vocation and the institution.

The Society for Human Resource Management and the Pew Research Center have both found that Black employees are more likely to leave employment than white employees.[11] Lack of opportunity for growth, lack of support, microaggressions, and other hazards—individual and systemic—that those from the margins face are real and not easily overcome, especially if vocation and institution are not aligned.[12] In fact, I, too, have found myself needing to change jobs to address these concerns. That said, without a doubt, in institutions where there was a deep and meaningful alignment between my vocation and the institution—regardless of whether I left—I could see the impact of my work and marginality on the institution.

What the Margins Frame

For many from the margins entering academia, there is a tendency to try to replicate the model of what success looks like in colleges and universities. Unfortunately, that model does not fit me, as a Black woman, and is unlikely to fit many other underrepresented populations. Like others, though, I tried mightily to fit that mold. What I eventually realized, however, was that the higher education model was not designed for me. I concluded that my success would be in spite of, not because of, the current model of higher education.

It was not until I recognized that what I had to offer was not my ability to be the same and mirror what higher education offers that I was able, instead, to see that it was my "difference" that would contribute to my work and help me fashion the institutions I cared very deeply about toward greater justice for all. In 2010, I wrote, "We have to explore those exclusionary traditions that hinder students from learning. We must stop trying to fit students to match a system that was never created for them and was, in fact, intended to discard or constrain them. Unless we begin to identify and reconfigure colleges and universities, we will continue to see large disparities between students because they are having largely disparate experiences. If we fail to rethink higher education, we will continue to replicate its inequities in increasing proportions."[13]

While these statements were written to support *student* success in higher education, the same principles apply to our institutional life and governance and the success of those who make up our institutions. We must look at the patterns and dynamics in higher education that exclude our personal contexts, that demand we separate our "soul and role," and that fracture our humanity and care for one another, and be willing to stand up to those structures and refuse to be a party to the injustice. Leaders of color may, like students, have disparate experiences from their majority colleagues because the institutions were not designed with them in mind. Unlike students, however, it is our *obligation* as professionals to impact those institutions in powerful ways to not only benefit ourselves but to benefit students as well. This impact can only be realized when we acknowledge the strength our context and vocation bring to our institutions. It was only when I was willing to embrace my "difference" and live authentically that I was able to truly engage colleagues in the work of diversity. It was the implementation of the Vocational Cycle to Support Institutional Justice that empowered me to make positive institutional changes. Whether through the development of curriculum review to support diversity, professional development to support diversity, or reviewing and implementing policies to support diverse hiring practices, this work was only accomplished successfully when I authentically engaged my institutions and allowed the cycle to unfold.

Use of the Vocational Cycle to Support Institutional Justice is imperative if we are going to bring about justice on our campuses. First, we must recognize and own the context that brought us forth and enable that context to shape our vocation. By being faithful to our vocation, we can make occupational choices that support institutional justice. These choices allow us to build on, learn from, and, when needed, challenge institutional life and governance structures. By bringing to bear the full weight of our vocation on these structures, we can refashion them in ways that positively and powerfully impact the institutional climate. That transformed climate then reshapes us, further enabling us to move forward with our work.

It is difficult to overstate the importance of being faithful to institutions and their work to create more just institutions. It is important not only so that people have equal employment access; it is equally important because it supports the hopes and dreams of the students on campus. However, if you discern a misalignment between your vocation and the institution, or if you feel that you are being targeted to a degree that compromises your well-being and vocation, it is also equally important that you know when to step back. The goal of the Vocational Cycle is not to create martyrs. Rather, it is to provide a framework for how your vocational commitments can support institutional transformation.

Questions for Reflection

For this chapter, it is important to go through each step of the cycle to see how your experience in the margins can inform your leadership around institutional change. Once you have considered each stage of the cycle, consider the following:

- How can the Vocational Cycle help amplify your leadership and sense of accomplishment at your institution?
- Are you currently engaging in activities that leave you divided? Why?
- What steps can you take to make new occupational choices based on your context and vocation?

PART III

The Margins Enhance

CHAPTER 8

Senior Leadership in Higher Education

In a recent conversation with an incoming college president, I was asked for my single best piece of advice. Without even a second's hesitation, the following emerged from my heart and my mouth: You have got to know who you are in order to know how you want to lead.

Without a doubt, when embarking on a leadership journey, you must think about what has led to the decision to be a leader, what assets you bring with you, and what weaknesses and challenges you must contend with. As shared throughout this book, the perceived barriers for leaders who hail from the margins are many. In fact, growing up in marginal spaces is often presented as something to overcome in order to be a leader, as opposed to viewing such leaders as having a uniquely valuable asset bank from which to draw. And yet, to lead, you must be clear about who you are—including your identities in the margins—and be willing to do the personal work consistently and intentionally.

But, leadership is about more than who you are as a person; for a senior leader in higher education, leadership is also very much about the institution. In this chapter, I discuss these competing notions: first, that leadership is not about you; and second, that leadership is all about you. I invite you, again, to wade through a dialectical opposition with me.

It's Not about You

One of the early lessons I learned in my first college presidency was a statement by Ed Pinson: "The president is not the presidency; the presidency is much larger than the president." In other words, no matter how vaunted the position, it's really not about you.

The mission of a college, or organization, or country, for that matter, is far bigger than any one leader. There are many who confuse and blend the president and the presidency. But the offices we hold existed long before we were ever born and will exist long after we have departed our roles. We are but one moment in time in a storied and important legacy, and that recognition is critical, publicly and privately. You are a steward. And to steward effectively, it's important to always focus on what binds our institution over time and across people. Without a doubt, as the leader you will encounter many people who you must lead and engage. Regardless of who you are personally, as a leader, it is important to properly engage with people as a representative of the office of the president, as the most visible reflection of the mission of the institution you serve.

I carry a phrase in my heart that I try to live daily: "I don't have to affirm the beliefs of everyone I encounter, but I do have to affirm their humanity." Again, these are not easy tasks. As a leader, you will encounter people with deep and affectionate ties to your institution, and with whom, nevertheless, you have deep disagreements. Sometimes people will say things with which I disagree. You will encounter people with whom you disagree or who have a belief system, political perspective, or way of being in the world that you are either unfamiliar with or with which you disagree. They may carry within their hearts understandings about the way the world works, who gets to have a voice in that world, or other crucial and consequential opinions that differ sharply from what's in your heart. Importantly, these differences may be tangled up with the work of improving equity within the institution. Perhaps your shared love for the institution will shrink the distance between you. But it may not. I'm not asking that you affirm everything in others' hearts, but I have learned that it is so important that we affirm the humanity of each person we encounter. Even when I vehemently disagree, I recognize that person is no less and no greater than myself, and I affirm their humanity.

As a leader, the privilege that you have is a great one, and you must deploy it intentionally and humanely. People will be watching you and learning from you in ways you never imagined. A very simple example is how people watch how I dress. While this has always been a tax on women, I have tried to use that to my advantage as the president. Every day, nearly without exception, for close to a decade, I have worn the primary colors of the institutions I have led: red at the College of Saint Benedict and green at Hollins University. I truly took to heart the notion of the president as the living logo of the institution. It's not that I especially prefer these colors, but they are a reminder that I serve something more than myself and my ego. By wearing these colors and taking pride in my institution, I have noticed (unscientifically) an uptick in the number of people who wear our school colors. This is a small example of the ways the leader sets the tone for the institution.

Of deeper consequence is how my students watch how I engage with them individually and with others. They search for and seek to understand how the leader regards students based on careful watching. The faculty, too, consists of keen observers who attach deep meaning to actions, and the governing board also looks to you for leadership and vision. Yes, that may be expected. But did you know that people also watch how you engage with your family or with your children? They look for an implied message that perhaps we didn't intend to share. This is without a doubt one of the most daunting parts of our roles. People are always watching how others, especially people from the margins, navigate life. We have to behave in such a way that when all eyes are on us, all of the people we represent, even if they disagree, would say we are representing the office, the institution, with integrity and decency and respect. Sometimes we all get frustrated, and we want to perhaps reveal parts of our baser instincts. But leaders do not have the luxury of doing that. At every move, we must affirm the mission of our institution. We must ensure that if a child is watching us, they believe they could be us. That is a weighty burden, and the greatest opportunity we have.

As you assume leadership roles, it is critically important that you think about how you want to engage with those who agree with you and those with whom you disagree. As a leader, you have many, often competing, constituents with whom you must engage. And you must engage with them in such a way that not only reflects who you are as the president, and as the chief proclaimer of the mission, but that reflects well on the presidency as an office, which is bigger than any individual.

For those of us on the margins, this, as with most things, is magnified. Yet, it also has the power to enhance your leadership. In fact, a willingness to speak out and use your platform can help to address the most intractable social issues we face. Drawing on past work by Joel E. Cohen and Adrianna Kezar, Eddie Cole and Shaun Harper found that "the choice of what is or is not said in presidential rhetoric determines what, or in this case who, is valuable (Cohen, 1995). This is important when considering the role of presidents in executing diversity agendas on campus. . . . [P]residents can be role models for how others can move a diversity agenda forward. Therefore, recognizing the individual or group targeted by a racial incident appears to be a valuable initial effort to bring them back into the broader campus community."[1]

As a leader, it is your job to use your platform and microphone to address these issues.

In many ways, dwelling in the margins prepares you for this work. While those of us on the margins are often ignored, we know that when a light is cast upon us, we must be prepared to respond. We know that our travels to the center are watched, often with a skeptical eye; therefore, we are keenly aware that we not only represent ourselves, but also all those in the margins with us.

As such, my leadership is not about me. I am a co-beneficiary and an inheritor of the missions and legacies I am privileged to steward as a president. I will never say it will be easy; I will never say you won't have doubt; I will never say it will be without struggle. But our leadership from the margins equips us to confront the demands of the office head-on. It equips us to face each of those things every day. We defy the odds. We do the impossible.

It's All about You

I introduced this chapter as a dialectic, and here's my foray into the contradiction. While leadership is about the institution, it is also very much about who you are as a person.

As shared in part I, the perceived barriers for leaders who hail from the margins are many. I recall a conversation I had with an executive coach early in my first presidency. She stated that the key to effective leadership is managing oneself. While this sounds easy, it is a daily challenge that demands ongoing learning and deep intentionality. Self-management requires that you have a clear vision and goals for yourself. That you have a learning agenda that you aggressively pursue and share with others. It means that you stand up for your institution and for yourself in challenging moments. It means that you know how and when to compromise and when to stand firm. In order to manage yourself and be a good leader, you must be clear about who you are and why you are in this role.

Central to the premise of this book is my belief that out of the margins is emerging a cadre of leaders and a strength of community that could only have been conceived in adversity. Courage is being born in those of us who might have once been turned away. Our voices, individually and collectively, are becoming clearer, louder, and more powerful. We are encouraging our communities to lean in to support and encourage one another. An educational leader I admire once said that people will sometimes draw a circle around themselves to exclude you. Our job, our mission, has to be to draw an even larger circle that includes us all. Those who may have once been excluded must make a conscious choice to reach out and include someone else. Your marginality and experiences are unique and make your leadership unique.

Many new college presidents spend their first year on a listening tour. I highly recommend that practice as a great way to learn not only about your institution, but also a great deal about yourself. I encourage you to reach out to those people who have had both positive and negative experiences at your institution and to learn from them. While you will hear both affirming and dissenting voices, you have the strength of dealing with dissension, having faced plenty from the center.

Without a doubt, it is challenging to talk with your detractors, especially those who view the margins as limiting, constraining, or othering. It is unfair that we have to use our energy to explain ourselves and our worldviews. I know what it is to walk into a room and be the only person who looks like me. I have been at conferences where there were over 400 people in the room and I was the only African-American woman in the room. I get that. But I also get that part of my task in this life is to walk into that room. To embrace my difference, and to speak my truth. I must speak it in a way that others can hear it. I have to speak it in a way that represents you well. That represents my family well. That is faithful to all the students, faculty, staff, and missions that I serve. I must speak it to my friends and to my enemies. I strive to speak my truth in such a way that were someone to listen, they couldn't tell who is, in fact, a friend and who is an enemy. And, as my former chief of staff reminded me, the challenge is sometimes about recognizing friends in a room when you are predisposed to see only enemies. It's about looking across difference and identifying friends when they look an awful lot like your enemies.

That's our task. It is a task that demands more from some of us than others. It is a task that will rely heavily on the work of allies. It is a task that on some days we may refuse to engage in out of a spirit of self-protection. But, to lead, we must do this uncomfortable work. So in the face of this discomfort, what should we do? How do we create a space and forum to bring us into a productive dialogue on our campuses? How do we expand the dialogue? Each one of us, regardless of our leadership role, must engage beyond our comfort zone.

So, What Is Leadership About?

As you discern leadership opportunities, it is essential that you think through the issues and values that are critical to your personal calling and vocation. As indicated in mission-driven leadership, it is essential that you align your work values with your heart values to lead effectively. Why does this matter if it's not about you? To effectively proclaim the mission of the institution you're charged with shepherding, it is important that you genuinely reflect and buy into those values. I have written previously about the deep resonance between my vocation and my institution, Hollins. An example from my first presidency at the College of Saint Benedict can illustrate how alignment between personal and institutional mission makes it possible to be a better leader.

During my six years as president at the College of Saint Benedict, I endeavored to learn all I could about its history, mission, and unspoken values. Critical to the college's identity was its founding by the Sisters of the Order of Saint Benedict. As a woman of color who, at the time, was not Catholic, I really wanted to find places of intersection in the spirit of the founders of the college and my own passions. To find the place where our commitments aligned. The sisters made that possibility very easy with their hospitality, but I also wanted to ensure that the alignment was strong.

In the summer of 2016, I was made aware of an 1899 ledger from Martin Loso's General Store and Harness Shop in St. Joseph, Minnesota. The ledger reflects a purchase of axle grease by the Sisters of Saint Benedict. My imagination surged as I thought about why the sisters needed axle grease. I eventually realized that the specifics surrounding the purchase were unimportant but that it was vitally important for me, and for College of Saint Benedict students, to know that our legacy began, in part, with axle grease.

You buy axle grease so you can get to work: building, fixing, planning, making life better. That's the legacy handed to the College of Saint Benedict by their founding order. That legacy directly aligns with my own personal legacy, despite demographic differences. I could see myself in their story. I believed the founders could find themselves in my story.

Decades ago, as the sisters charted their way forward and today, at moments when today's students from the margins are questioned and challenged, I knew there were questions the founders then, and I today, faced: Are you certain? Are you worthy? Are you sure, as young women, that you should do this? Then and now, we look people in the eye and answer yes. *Yes, I'm certain. Yes, I'm worthy. Yes, we can do this.* The Sisters of Saint Benedict were determined to change their trajectory, even as they found themselves, like I find myself, in the margins.

As you can see, there was a deep alignment between the founding mission and values of the College of Saint Benedict, Hollins University, and my own experiences and purposes in this life. That alignment made it possible for me to lead from a position of strength, to effectively steward the institutional missions and make the president's work about the institution. That deep alignment is critical to your success professionally, and personally, that alignment is critical to help you move beyond the very valuable defiance you may have developed in the margins.

What the Margins Frame

The defiance I learned as I assumed my first college presidency—the axle-grease legacy that sustains the College of Saint Benedict—was an easy fit for my personal leadership style. My return to the South to lead Hollins University and students whose backgrounds were often very similar to my own was also very much a personal alignment with what matters most in my life. But, as I thought about my personal and professional mission and purpose, I had to consider what it means to grow as a leader and to begin to encourage others from the margins. I didn't want the overwhelming resonance between the College of Saint Benedict or Hollins University and my own sense of defiance to limit where and how I can lead. I had to shift my own thinking about desire in order to help other communities think through what they desire for themselves, in their own contexts.

For example, when all needs are met, what do you desire? And, by definition, shouldn't those desires be bigger than the self? Shouldn't they be focused on how one can contribute to the common good? When one can meet every desire, then is the goal to think through not only what one deserves, but how one can help and support others in achieving and receiving what they deserve? Perhaps in other contexts deserving becomes more about responsibility and obligation. When we have all we desire, what responsibility do we have toward others? While my orientation and experience were born in defiance, I believe that my purpose of creating equity resonates with desire and deserving, even as the work goes beyond the internal to addressing external obligations.

My life has shifted so that it is no longer about me and defiance; it's about desiring to make a larger contribution and recognizing that *what I deserve* is to frame my life and work in order to help others achieve what they deserve. I didn't publicly articulate this idea until the spring of 2022 when someone in a leadership academy posed the question, "How did you know you had made it?"

To be honest, this question stunned me. As I said when I began my rambling answer, it had never occurred to me that I had "made it." I was not even sure what "making it" would mean. While I was proud of the work I had done, I had never paused to think about making it. In fact, my initial answer was insufficient, explaining that, like the gospel song, my living will not be in vain if I have helped somebody. While this is true, it was, at best, an unsatisfactory answer. I asked the questioner to bear with me and to give me a little time to ponder my answer.

After several minutes of thinking and responding to other questions, a moment when I felt like I had made it suddenly crystallized for me. The date was September 29, and I was a sitting president at the time. People about whom I cared deeply—and who I think cared deeply about me—asked me to participate in a process which I felt was fraught. The process was not unethical, illegal, or in any way untoward. But, it would have required me to re-prove and defend myself as a leader—in a way that I didn't think a white man would have been asked. I felt strongly that were I to participate in this process, I would be undermining my own value, my years of hard work, my leadership, and all the people who stood in the margins alongside me. I would have sacrificed a core piece of who I am and my own mission had I gone along with the request. So, I said no. And while I had said no in many other instances, this was the first time I said no in support of my espoused beliefs, my purpose, and my integrity, and did not feel guilty about it. I recall the joyful experience of finally protecting myself and my values in the face of opportunity. This was the moment when I felt like I had made it.

At last, it was time for my defiance to give way to something else. While the anger implicit in defiance had been an important motivator as I assumed a leadership role, I needed something more to look toward long-term. I had moved beyond my need for defiance and risked misusing my current access and privilege by continuing to lead from that place. Might it be time for my defiance to refashion itself into something different? Should I now use my position to focus less on defiance and more on desire?

This shift means moving from a life and leadership stance crafted in response to others, to a life and leadership stance in response to my own observations of what the world needs and demands. What do I desire to see accomplished in the world? How can I begin to define my actions myself, not in response to the world's continually low expectations of me? Perhaps the second half of my life should not be defined by what I lack and don't have access to but what I desire to do because of the access my defiance has created.

This shift is difficult. It demands that I reimagine my gaze from the expectations of others and say clearly, and for myself, what I want. This has repercussions far beyond me. How do I move institutions from a defiance mindset (we will survive despite everything) to a desire mindset (this is who we want to be in the world)? How do I understand my leadership from a proactive perspective of what I want and intend to change in the world, as opposed to a reactive mindset (I can fix this)?

To shift to intentionally dwelling in the land of desire as opposed to defiance requires a new skill set. A skill set that recognizes one has the access, means, resources, and skills to bring to fruition one's desires. Desire recognizes that there is privilege involved; I can think about what I want in addition to what I need. Desire requires constant monitoring to ensure I am not focusing only on personal wants but also fulfilling an obligation to the world.

And, desire requires one think carefully about what one deserves. If the mindset is one of lacking—that one doesn't deserve happiness, success, peace, comfort—then one's desires will simply remain that, desires, and fail to become realized. To work toward one's desires, one must believe in their right to those things. The world, even in 2023, says I deserve very little. I desire to create a world where little girls grow up believing differently.

This notion of speaking up for and pursuing what one deserves also translates to the *troubled landscape of higher education*. We in higher education are often told that what we do has no real value. That we, and our institutions, are entitled and irrelevant. To succeed in our work, we have to say: We deserve funding, and support, and to survive. What we believe about our mission—that educating students to ask difficult questions and craft thoughtful answers has real value—is fundamentally true. We have the right to demand society's attention and support because *we are deserving*. And our desires—to enroll more students, to find funding and support to help us with that mission—are legitimate desires.

Finally, and importantly, one must distinguish between deserving access to work toward something and feeling entitled to it. There are few things less attractive and less compelling than a sense of entitlement. The reality is the world still wants to tell me what I can and cannot do, who I can and cannot be, what I should and shouldn't want for myself and for others. My desire is to speak back to that in such a way that my actions and the things I undertake reflect desire and make a clear statement that no matter what the world says, I deserve to see myself as successful, as a leader, and I can craft my desires to work toward that goal.

So perhaps there is one last act of defiance in me. To defy myself and my inclination to second-guess my right to these things. To defy my tendency to think I don't deserve to have desires, which is just another way of being placed in a box—a box I have already defied my way out of.

How can we shape what we feel we deserve for ourselves, in our own voice? As leaders, how will we articulate and act on our desires? The balance between personal and institutional mission isn't found overnight, and the leap from defiance to desire to deserving doesn't unfold in one fell swoop. And, in my own leadership journey, it took a larger test to see if I was ready for "deserving." I get to that in the next chapter.

Questions for Reflection

- In what ways have you conflated the office you hold with who you are as a leader? Are there places you need to create space?
- How have your marginal identities uniquely equipped you for your work ahead?

- What do you desire for yourself and for the common good? What do you desire to see accomplished in the world?
- How do you frame your leadership from a proactive perspective rather than a reactive mindset? How can you begin to define your actions for yourself, not in response to the world's expectations?

CHAPTER 9

On Courage and Gratitude

In the Talmud, we find the teaching, "Do not be daunted by the enormity of the world's grief. Do justly now, love mercy now, walk humbly now. You are not obligated to complete the work, but neither are you free to abandon it." The recognition that we must continue the work, even—especially—when we are daunted, is a profound one. Each day as a leader, you can likely find a formidable task or situation. How does one decide to continue the work in the face of such challenges? How are leaders from the margins uniquely equipped to do this work? It is my experience that leaders from the margins have developed a unique level of courage born out of their experiences. Alongside that courage comes a profound sense of gratitude that enables leaders from the margins to not only refuel their wells of courage but allows them to support the leadership of others. This chapter explores both courage and gratitude and why (and how) they matter for leaders from the margins.

On Courage

In 2020, I received the Courageous Leader Award from Credo, a tremendous honor and recognition of my leadership. It was truly unexpected and, I felt at times, unmerited. Receiving this award was an external affirmation of my leadership by a group I truly admired. It was as if I had been seen, heard, and valued for embracing leadership and the margins. However, I have long wrestled with what it means to be a leader, much less a courageous leader. I have consistently explored what made me decide to become vulnerable to the challenges of leadership and what gives me courage now.

Having spent much of my career in Catholic higher education, it should come as no surprise that I went back to the Latin origins of these words to figure out what they mean. Allow me to quickly dispense with the Latin for *leader*, for which there are multiple translations. Since it's already in my title, I decided to go with *doctor*, which connotes leader and guide. There are other translations, for example, princeps or rector, but there's great consistency to the meaning. I find myself clinging to the idea that a leader is a guide as opposed to a chief, general, or captain. I like to think of a leader as one who shepherds a group, helping to fashion their journey and path but also helping to shape the group's experience. I delight in that notion.

The word *courageous* derives from the Latin word *couer*, or heart. As I grew up reading about leaders and what makes a good leader, I didn't hear much about the heart. In fact, much of the leadership development theory I was exposed to seemed to go out of its way to say that you must be objective, cold, unemotional, and stalwart to be a leader. I was told that leadership is a lonely job, and you must command respect. I didn't grow up thinking of a leader, especially not a courageous leader, as someone who guides from the heart. However, as I think about what a courageous leader means, I begin to believe that "one who guides from the heart" might be a compelling way to define the phrase.

While I haven't seen the word *heart* used in many leadership theories, there is now an emergence of the value of connected, compassionate leadership. Chapter six goes into deeper detail about this, but as a reminder, there has been a significant amount of recent literature focusing on emotional intelligence and the importance of authentic, engaged leadership. And, I will say, I do know that leadership requires that you do certain things from the heart. Things which, perhaps, require courage. So, to lead courageously is, to some degree, about the choice to lead with the heart.

To be a leader, I have learned that you must have the courage—the heart—to listen to your team. I have repeatedly said that a leader is only as good as the people they surround themselves with. And, if you're surrounded by good people—as I have had the uncanny privilege to be throughout my career—then you must actively seek out and listen to their counsel. With the people with whom you are closest, the people who are with you in the arena, and the people who stand alongside you in good times and bad, you must have the courage to listen to their counsel and act on it. Yes, that does take some level of courage, as there's this mythology that the leader is on their own, but in my experience, I am a much, much better leader because of the people around me, not despite them.

What this means, though, is that you must have the courage—the heart—to be vulnerable with your team and with your community. That feels risky, just saying it out loud. You have to be human, be real, and be fallible with the people you have the privilege of guiding. You cannot lead if you are living a divided life as a human in private and pseudo-superhero in public. You cannot effectively do this work compartmentalizing your truth from your role or your vulnerability from your courage. Your vulnerability—your humanity—is what allows you to make the difficult decisions and garner the support of your community. Because they know you care. Because they know you, too, are impacted. In fact, to be courageous without vulnerability risks being cruel.

Inherent in that premise is the notion that you know your community and they know you. As a leader, you must have the courage—the heart—to form a relationship with the people you are guiding. Just because someone is slower on the path or complaining about the way forward doesn't mean you get to walk away from them. It's at those moments when your relationship matters even more. You have to be a fellow sojourner. You must be a partner, not just a leader.

I have learned these lessons and stand by them. I have become comfortable guiding with my heart—a heart that, I confess, often asks for data. But first, my heart tries to see the hopes, the fears, and the calling in others. I recognize that by helping others be their best selves, our entire community is better and stronger.

And yet, I still find myself uncomfortable with the nomenclature of *courageous leader*. I think it's because, while I believe and endeavor daily to live as a sojourner, a partner, and a data-informed shepherd, I know that my leadership comes not by my choice but by my calling. Like many leaders from the margins, if I am courageous, it's not because I choose to be. It's because I must be. When I think about myself, there's some degree to which I don't have a choice. I did not choose this. I was called to it.

Here's what I mean. To do some of the most fundamental parts of this work requires that I do things that no rational person would likely choose. I still all too often have to gather up my courage—activate my heart—to do the simplest things. For example, when I must walk into a room where I am the only person of color and realize both the extraordinary privilege and exquisite inequity in that moment, I know that my calling demands that I be in that room. My work is there, but my presence signals not courage but fulfilling my call, doing what I must even when that action brings forth pain. My heart still twists when I recall my first Council of Independent Colleges (CIC) Presidents' Institute when "colleagues" asked me repeatedly how I managed to become a college president, when the restaurant refused to serve me, and when I was confused with hotel staff and asked to take care of the coats. I doubt that I will ever forget these events. The way my stomach dropped when a colleague I had met before and greatly admired turned around to me in the registration line and asked if I could take her coat. When I said, no, that I was waiting for registration, I was greeted with a sniff, and with the haughtiest tone possible, my colleague replied, "Well, what school are you from, and what are you doing here?" While I will likely always remember that encounter, I have seen this colleague many times since that exchange, and I don't think they recall how cavalierly they dismissed me. My work is to not let what was, for them, an offhand remark to someone who was largely invisible to them shape how I understand myself.

I would not choose to be made to feel less than nor will I define myself by that. While some may call my leadership amid these circumstances courageous, I see it as an act of defiance. It was my work to fulfill my calling so the next generation doesn't experience that same hurt. Like many leaders from the margins, I call it merely trying to affirm my own and others' humanity when I have to speak out against injustice, fight for equity, keep talking about inclusion, and justify the unique value of women's education. This part of my work is exhausting, a level of exhaustion no one would choose, but this exhaustion must be embraced if it's what you are called to do. Or, as a study entitled "Beating the Odds" indicated, "In a sense, their race and gender put these women under a spotlight, and that can be exhausting. Some described it as a kind of tax—one that majority employees don't have to pay, and one that could easily derail a career."[1]

I must lead with my heart when I speak up and act, not because I am necessarily courageous but because there are many wonderful ways of being in the world, all of which are valuable and worthy of exploration, even if they aren't traditional.

So, if I have any courage, it was born of the necessity to just be myself in a world where that's not always enough. If I am courageous, it is because I had to be just to stand up, just to exist. And once you stand up for yourself, as many leaders from the margins must do, you must, and you feel equipped to, stand up for others.

The beauty of dwelling in the margins is that I know that I am not alone in these experiences. To all who have likewise struggled, who have felt dismissed, who have felt diminished, who have felt defeated, know that you are not alone. Recognize that your calling to activate your heart is bigger than all else. Your effort to advocate, support, and sustain yourself and others is not unnoticed. Your calling guides your heart. And, by definition, that makes you a courageous leader.

For me, being a courageous leader means having the courage—the heart—to surrender to my calling and to realize each day that there is work to be done and that I must do it with all my heart.

On Gratitude

While I recognize the importance of courage as a leader, I am also fully aware that leadership, especially in relationships, demands a healthy degree of gratitude. You see, it was the support, encouragement, and kindness of many people that made me a leader. If anything I have done can be labeled as courageous, it is a byproduct of the work of my community and support that emboldened me. Therefore, I think it is important to frame a conversation about gratitude in the larger context of sponsorship and mentoring, including why sponsors and mentors matter and deserve gratitude.

Both *mentorship* and *sponsorship* play a critical role in developing all leaders. Mentorship is defined as "a mutually beneficial professional relationship in which an experienced individual (the mentor) imparts knowledge, expertise, and wisdom to a less experienced person (the mentee)."[2] Sponsorship takes that relationship further: in addition to sharing knowledge and expertise with you, a sponsor advocates and acts for you.

Research about sponsors and sponsorship first gained momentum in conversations about women's leadership. While we know that women are less likely to have access to sponsors than men, we also know that the presence of sponsors benefits women's leadership. For women of color, we find that having a community of support is essential. As an article in the *Harvard Business Review* states, "it wasn't simply personal strengths and talents that got them there. It was the willingness and ability of others to recognize, support, and develop those strengths and talents."[3]

We note a similar phenomenon on the corporate side, as Korn Ferry reports:

> They say that if you want to go fast, you should go alone, but if you want to go far, you should go together. Holding true to this adage, most of the Black leaders (86 percent) in our study said that sponsors were essential to their career progression. These Black leaders made a conscious decision to be visible and gain exposure with their advocates—and to offer these advocates value. In turn, the sponsors opened doors, provided exposure and advocated for these Black leaders, which helped them build relationships, access new opportunities and advance their careers.[4]

It was the presence of mentors and sponsors that made a tremendous difference from the earliest moments of my career to today. Like many on the margins, and as shared in chapter three, I was told that my efforts were not merely for myself. I needed to undertake this work for others as well. In Holmes' study exploring the experiences of African-American presidents, she writes:

> The other presidents spoke of how their parents and extended family members encouraged them to be focused in high school so that their grades would permit them to gain admission into college. They spoke of the encouragement they received from their pastors, church members, and leaders in the community. One female president said, "Everyone was always telling me to do the best I could in school so that I could go to college and make something of myself. My accomplishments are really a testimony

of all of those people back in my hometown." The presidents also believed this network of people instilled in them a drive to succeed despite the adverse conditions some of them grew up in, as well, as the acts of discrimination they often encountered. Another male president indicated that his father told him repeatedly to "learn how to work with your mind so you won't have to use your hands to earn a living like me."[5]

I cannot overstate the power of sponsors early in my life. In fact, it was a kind act—an act we would now label as sponsorship—that transformed my life. You'll recall in chapter one, I explained the crushing disappointment that I faced when I was told by a guidance counselor that Black women do not attend college. My mother went to her employers, Betty and Marshall Cooper, shared my story, and asked for help. Without hesitation, the Cooper family paid for me to attend Saint Mary's School as a boarding student. Had they not engaged in this degree of sponsorship, I have no doubt that I would not be here today. The only condition of their support was that I had to work hard, and they always assured me that they knew I would do so. Mrs. Cooper is still a prominent figure in my life, a woman who has never been afraid to speak her mind and who has always been generous in her love and creating opportunity for others.

While Mr. and Mrs. Cooper were my first sponsors, they were far from my last. In college, it was my undergraduate advisor, Dr. Laurie Heatherington. Laurie taught a section of my very first psychology class, and I met her on my first or second day at Williams. She was funny and exuded warmth. She told a very funny, somewhat self-deprecating story to start class, and I remember thinking two things: I want to know her, and I want to be her. She was clearly a strong woman, but you could feel—even in a lecture course—how deeply she cared. Laurie and her husband, Keith Finan, took me in and encouraged me. Laurie allowed me to be her teaching assistant and listened carefully to my ideas and feedback. She helped me to believe that my ideas had value and merited being taken seriously. With Laurie, it was easy to be smart and want to engage with the life of the mind because she made me feel worthy of that. She was also a powerful role model of what it meant to be a woman who worked a great deal and raised a family. She showed me that it's okay to be a woman and have deep ambition. She raged with me against the notion that, for women, motherhood had to come before all else. The first time I ever heard her use an expletive was when the show *Murphy Brown* had Murphy leave work to raise her child. While certainly a worthy choice, it felt like a public rebuke to all the women who made a different choice. Laurie was outraged and allowed me to lean into her outrage with her. Once in the professional world, these early sponsors, occasional mentors, and lessons helped me navigate as a professional and a leader.

My ascension in higher education would not have happened without support from many people along the way. As Waring writes in her study of African-American women leaders:

> The presidents report that they joined the administrative ranks in one of two ways. Either because they were "drafted" by others who identified their leadership potential and helped to develop it. Or, they were interested in improving the educational opportunities for students, primarily minority students, and took administrative positions where they felt they could have an impact. Regardless of their method of entry into administration, their subsequent hard work and record of success propelled them steadily upward. What

they shared, to a large degree however, was a general initial reluctance to become "leaders."[6]

I was indeed reluctant, as I did not see myself as a president and did not give it much consideration early in my academic career. I felt that I needed to serve others as closely as possible and thought that meant remaining in non-leadership roles. Ultimately, I was drafted into administrative work by the first president I served, Michael MacDowell. Even then, however, as I began to see the outlines of higher education leadership, I still did not see myself as a higher education leader nor did I have those aspirations. Had it not been for a mentor-turned-sponsor, I would not be a college president. It was Father Kevin Mackin, OFM, who brought to life, and actively sponsored, my becoming a college president. Fr. Kevin had served as president of many institutions by the time I met him. While active with the Franciscan Order, he was also a wonderful and highly engaged college president.

I had the privilege of serving Fr. Kevin at Mount Saint Mary College in Newburgh, New York. This was Fr. Kevin's third presidency, and he taught me—as a mentor and sponsor—many things. His deep student engagement and commitment to student success are things I attempt to emulate in my own leadership. His excellence with fundraising sets a high bar for me as well. But Fr. Kevin also modeled what it means to invest in another. Without lots of lecturing or philosophical reflection, Fr. Kevin simply told me to do those things that would set me apart and prepare me for a presidency. We never discussed my reluctance; instead, he focused on my preparation. Out of his own resources, he sent me to "fundraising school" and the Harvard Institute for Educational Management, opportunities I would not have been able to afford on my own. He allowed me to walk alongside him as he visited donors. He was frank with me when issues arose and taught me how to think about technical and contractual parts of this world. He showed me what it meant to be an unapologetic leader.

I can still clearly recall the day Fr. Kevin brought the College of Saint Benedict presidential posting to my office and told me to apply. I demurred many, many times, but the urgency with which he encouraged me eventually won. It was Fr. Kevin who made me realize that I could do this despite my reluctance. I will never forget that or take it for granted.

What the Margins Frame

The role of mentors and sponsors I describe is not uncommon in the leadership of people from the margins. Jackson and Harris write:

> Vaughan (1989) reported that key role models and mentors are major influences for women seeking leadership positions. Hart (1995) identified that those with mentors are more likely to have a job offer for university faculty and senior administration. Findings in this study also verified the importance of a mentor in the ascension to the presidency. Thirty-five percent of the presidents reported that a mentor affected their current presidency.[7]

Similarly, for leaders from the margins, it is critical to serve in those mentoring and sponsorship roles for the next generation of leaders from the margins. Because we know the professional and personal importance of such leadership support, it is critical that leaders from the margins intentionally take on this work.

The margins are also an extraordinary place to learn both courage and gratitude. While courageous skills are often dismissed, it takes great courage to speak up and advocate for oneself and one's needs in the margins. It takes courage to be able to support a family and to attain an education in a world that seeks to dismiss or erase you. It takes deep courage to keep moving forward once you have encountered multiple entrenched systems designed to hold you back. It is pure courage that provides the resilience to keep moving forward with integrity and success even when perched on a glass cliff.

Likewise, gratitude is deeply imbued in the margins. Gratitude to those in the margins with whom we dwell is critically important. Therefore, when I think about leadership and gratitude, I am fully aware that I have much to be grateful for and even more to give back.

Questions for Reflection

- Who are your mentors? Who are your sponsors?
- Who can you ask to mentor or sponsor you?
- Who can you mentor or sponsor?

CHAPTER 10

Interrogating the Demands
of the Margins

I began envisioning this chapter at a high-top table at the open-ing reception for inductees into the American Academy of Arts and Sciences. I was one of the inductees, and as I stood under a tent with several other Academy members, I suddenly found my-self questioning everything—my accomplishments, my worthi-ness, and this book. In that moment, I felt like the margins had failed me. I felt that I had no right to this place, that I was not prepared, and that I did not belong in the room. I was, in that moment, standing in the center of the center, a bright light shin-ing on me, and I felt like an interloper.

This feeling was different than imposter syndrome, the diag-nosis that pathologizes almost universal feelings of discomfort and self-doubt in the workplace. I did not feel like a fraud. I felt, even among the most welcoming of people who were honoring

The "Hope in the Margins" section in this chapter is adapted from Mary Dana Hinton, "The Whisper of Dangerous Memory." *Interfaith America*, May 17, 2022. https://www.interfaithamerica.org/the-whisper-of-dangerous-memory. Used with permission.

me for my achievements, that I did not belong. In that moment, I felt that by being in the center, I had betrayed my fidelity to the margins, and I had lost a significant part of my identity. I wasn't pretending to be someone else; I was wrestling with my authentic identity.

Add to that the fact that it was clear those systems that make me seek the margins remained vibrantly at play. It was clear that I was one of the marginalized in the room. The very systems and structures that led to this august occasion had once been fashioned to hold me, and people like me, at bay. At times, among some, there was even a whiff of questioning as to how I made it to this point. I am often asked, "How did you get your job?" by others in similar positions. The way the question is framed and the frequent follow-up "Are you an alum?" seem to imply that I somehow evaded the rigorous process leading to a presidency. Those questions were asked in this space. Additionally, the institutional hierarchy we often seek to ignore in higher ed was at play. Of course, by ignoring the hierarchy, we leave it unchallenged, which only serves to reinforce it.

While fear and doubt rushed over me, I began to consider what I had written in this book, what I would say to a new leader who asked me how to handle such a situation, and I realized that is the very premise of the book. You will have moments when you feel excluded, othered, and unworthy, but you must take a step back and remember the unique strengths you bring to this gathering. So, that's what I did, and it's what I encourage you to do, too.

As I gathered my wits about me, I realized that this was not the most challenging room I had ever entered. I started entering rooms where I felt unwelcome, unseen, and unvalued as early as elementary school. In some of these rooms, I did not just feel that I did not belong; I was actively unwanted. I have spent time in spaces that were literally built by my ancestors, who were treated as chattel in their own lifetimes and erased from collective memory in subsequent years. My being within these spaces prompts a dangerous memory—a reminder of the suffering, despair, perseverance, courage, and hope that built these spaces occupied so comfortably by those in the center.[1]

You, too, have entered challenging rooms. That is the strength that you call upon. Think about your first time in a room where you felt uncertain, concerned, and doubtful. Perhaps it will never be easy to enter those center spaces, but you enter them because it will, with practice, get easier. And, even more, you will learn how to reimagine and influence those spaces so that others on the margins—and those in the center—feel welcomed, heard, seen, and valued. This experience—along with many others I had forgotten in the moment—has helped me learn to use my marginality to create those other spaces. To facilitate traveling between the margins and the center. To make the world better.

As I pondered these thoughts at that high-top table under the tent, I realized that there are several other messages that I should share as you take your own journey between the margins and the center, a journey that is not unidirectional but circular. A journey that perhaps gets easier with each cycle. A journey that, like all journeys, brings with it highs and lows, wins and losses. It is a journey that you do not take alone. You are accompanied by many: ancestors who came before you, those in the margins who have locked arms with you, and allies in the center who honor and support you.

Early Presidential Leadership Lessons

As I mentioned earlier, when I first became a college president, I had the good fortune of working with executive coach Annie McKee. Without equivocation, I encourage all emerging and current leaders to work with a coach. It is invaluable to have an external person who can help you identify problems and blind spots and support truly open brainstorming. In addition, it is important to have someone who you can come to with your biggest professional concerns without fear of judgment and with the hope of growth. I chose Annie based on her book *Resonant Leadership*,[2] as I found myself, my leadership style, and my leadership goals in alignment with the book. I was very fortunate that Annie ultimately agreed to be my coach.

My initial work with Annie revolved around her helping me have the confidence to walk into a room that I suspected would be, at best, lonely and, at worst, hostile: a room of my peers, college presidents, at an annual presidential convening. My prior experiences with my peers had not always been welcoming. All too often, I would get questions and comments like, "How did you get your job?" or "What are you doing here?" or "Well, you must be an alum to be in that presidency." Or, as happened more than once, I would be asked if I could take coats or point people to the bathroom. Some of my colleagues most certainly did not see me as a peer and did not treat me as such. That took a toll on my confidence and my willingness to use my voice.

So, for two months, Annie and I worked on my own internal narrative as well as ways I could respond when this annual event came around. I jokingly say that Annie taught me how to walk into a room. In all seriousness, Annie taught me how to believe in myself, my voice, my vision, and my mission in any room. She did this by helping me learn to turn to my strengths, strengths born in the margins, strengths that equipped me to walk into those rooms and speak back to those who seek to diminish me with their words. That is my goal for each of you: own who you are and trust that you are needed in those rooms to bring your perspective to the world.

I want to conclude by sharing two important leadership tactics that she shared with me. First, early in our coaching relationship, Annie shared that a critical part of being a leader is managing yourself. I wasn't sure what this meant, so Annie helped me understand that how I related to others and how I presented myself in terms of what I cared about, responded to, and gave my attention to signaled what type of leader I am and whether people could trust me.

Roughly translated, some could say this leadership advice speaks to not flying off the handle and always being "presidential." That's not a wrong interpretation, but it is an incomplete interpretation. Managing yourself means taking the time to be introspective about what type of leadership is needed, by whom, and when. It's about asking yourself questions regarding what you must know and be able to do to be an effective leader. It's about taking the time to critically reflect on the decisions you made and why you made them. It's about thinking through what must be done today and how to create a legacy of leadership that you would be proud of. This advice has been priceless to me and has forced me to be clear about my mission and leadership. I often think about whether I am managing myself well. Before I can lead—or even manage others—I first must manage myself.

The second piece of advice, and I can hear Annie's voice as I type this, was, "Saying thank you is a complete sentence." As I have referenced in other sections, owning my voice and leadership did not come easy to me. I often wrestled with feeling unworthy. Before I learned the value of the margins, I thought that I needed to explain away my past or compensate for it. When people would laud my leadership or say something kind, my tendency was to explain it away. To demur.

But one day, Annie asked me what would happen if I just said thank you. We practiced me just saying thank you. Learning to say thank you and stop speaking is an incredible gift. It signals to the person that you heard them, and it signals to yourself to slow down and receive the kind words being offered. In the silence after the thank you, you get to enjoy the human exchange of gratitude. Learn to say thank you and be quiet. And yes, I still have to practice.

Continued Lessons from the Margins

In my decade as a college president, I have continued to add to those early leadership tools Annie shared with me. Many of my leadership lessons have come from my experience in the margins, as will yours.

You should know that you will, as I just have, continue to find situations that are challenging, situations where you question your margins and may, by default, want to pretend to be in the center. That happens, and sometimes you may engage in that pretense. However, be aware that even if you lose sight of your mission and goal, you can find your way back. Your mission, your authentic self, your North Star: that is your core. Yes, you may wander away at times, but if you listen to the voice that whispers with integrity, you will find your way back. When you do, you will have even more strength and courage in your arsenal for the next stage of the journey.

This is the great, inescapable, central gift of the leader from the margin. We all need to learn that each of us can be (and must become) sufficient within ourselves. That we are, in our individuality, good enough as we are. This truth can be hard to grasp for someone who never had to confront the ugly experience of being described as (or viewed as) less than what was required. Even those from communities of privilege can encounter this diminishing assessment: *You can't do this job; you're too frail. Or too soft. Your mental illness makes you too unreliable. Your sympathies for your employees are a weakness.* A leader who has come to realize that she is sufficient despite the world telling her she is insufficient is more likely to see the value of employees who openly struggle or otherwise reveal their normal day-to-day frailties.

There is little need, room, or utility in viewing yourself—in the margins or the center—as a martyr. Being in the margins— or even being marginalized—should not require one to sacrifice joy. You are not being called to self-sacrifice for the world. Rather, you are being called to enhance, inform, and transform the world but not at the expense of your own well-being. I believe that it is easy for those of us on the margins—perhaps especially women—to fall into this trap. We are socialized to believe that we must sacrifice ourselves, our wants, and even our needs to better others. Kate Manne wrote, "Her humanity may hence be held to be owed to other human beings, and her value contingent on her giving moral goods to them: life, love, pleasure, nurture, sustenance, and comfort, being some such."[3] Women, and many of us on the margins, are rarely afforded the opportunity to just be. Rather, we are taught to sacrifice for others, to always give back, and to put the community's needs ahead of our own, always. As someone with a service orientation, this resonates with me. However, one's service and commitment to others in the margins are not paid for with your physical, emotional, mental, and spiritual wellness. The margins don't demand that of you.

The margins ask that you recognize you have a role in the betterment of society—a role not determined or proscribed by the center—but the margins don't say you have to lose yourself to fill that role. When you cross the line from servant-leader to martyr, you are feeding the narrative that you must give up yourself and what you deserve as a human being to fit societal views of who you should be—a human sacrifice. As noted earlier, you have the right to move beyond defiance and the right to demand more and better. You are also worthy of being able to identify and lean into what you desire in life. You deserve to live into your truth and your calling. The center may insist that those in the margins are undeserving. You deny that narrative by recognizing that you have a right to deserve more.

On the flip side, it's also important for you to acknowledge the, at times fleeting, privilege that you may be afforded or encounter as a leader. Yes, those in margins can find themselves with incredible privilege in certain spaces and at certain times. For example, as you ascend in leadership roles, you will find increasing economic privilege and social mobility. In your community, you may find yourself with great social privilege. These privileges do not cancel out your marginality, as privilege is rarely static for those of us from the margins. (While I may be able to afford more things economically, I am still treated with skepticism when I enter stores.) However, ignoring economic privilege is not the solution. Similarly, to pretend to never have experienced privilege is to be inauthentic.

The call is to dwell in the tension between having inhabited the margins and choosing to be there with the current reality of having access to, while refuting, the center. This is a challenging tension to live in, and it requires great clarity about why you're in the space.

At the American Academy of Arts and Sciences event, and in so many spaces in the past, I've sought the people I perceive as "like me" in some way: another lone woman, another lone Black person, another person whose face belies their feelings of discomfort. Those of us from the margins find and support each other; we create little islands of belonging within the lonely ocean that is the center. Most often, the people I perceive as "like me" are not really much like me at all, but our shared marginality is enough. I am grateful for their support when the demands of the margins feel overwhelming.

It is one type of challenge when you find yourself feeling adrift while looking for support. But, in truth, I've spent more time throughout my leadership journey considering what to do when seeming friends and allies offer the greatest challenge. So, let's turn to how to cope with friendly fire.

Coping with Friendly Fire

"Shallow understanding from people of good will is more frustrating than absolute misunderstanding from people of ill will."
—MARTIN LUTHER KING, Jr.[4]

Amid the challenges of leadership, what enables me to get out of bed in the morning is my unrelenting belief in the goodness of humankind. While I know intellectually that there are people of ill will in the world, I would find it personally incapacitating if I focused on that group of people. I could not get up in the morning if I questioned the motives of everyone I encounter. So,

I know from the outset that those in the center are people of good will. Your allies and friends are people of good will, but one of the demands of the margins is that you recognize and demand more than good will from those around you.

To be clear, people of good will are essential to supporting equity and justice. When any oppressed or marginalized group begins to seek equity, the majority population is an essential and important ally. When you live in an environment of inequity, discomfort, or even hate and begin to seek justice, those people who provide even a glimmer of kindness are so rare—and so important to the cause—that they are welcomed. When you live your life feeling less than or so unlike others, to be seen as a full human being is a veritable life jacket when you're drowning. A kind word and a smile become evidence of your humanity. When your daily life is lived under assault, good will is so rare that it's all you ask for. Your earliest allies are people of eager good will who reach out to you.

But, as we make small gains toward social justice, large gains become an inevitable goal. Why should I settle for a portion of justice when I deserve full equity? Those who provide good will are then asked for more than a smile: How will you support my humanity when your mere presence is no longer enough? Will you be invested in my well-being when there may be a cost to you? Will you sacrifice your comfort to be a witness to my humanity? When people are fed up with the calling out of injustice, how do we shift concerns from personal impact to concern about why the injustice happened? How do we move the focus from fret and concern about the need to change to being more self-critical so that we can grow? How do we hear from others whose experiences may be dramatically different from our own? How do we hear new truths about our culture? Just because it's not the truth we want, just because it's not our experience, does not mean it is not true or didn't happen. How can we hear those truths in a way that binds us as opposed to alienating us?

These are the questions that those of us from the margins must ask as we engage the center. Perhaps the margins demand that we see each other as more than a monolith, more than one-dimensional people. Every person is complex and deep and wants their full humanity seen and witnessed. Every single person. When we extend that to everyone around us, we must begin to translate that to systems that support humanity. We must do the deep work of cultural change that enables fluidity between the center and the margins. The margins demand such.

In higher education, this is the work of learning institutions. Leaders from the margins are uniquely equipped to help institutions with marginal traits like vulnerability, openness, and the goal of creating systems that honor humanity. We can support institutions in learning this work and embedding it in what we do, the policies we create, and the environments we establish.

Engaging in Micro-Progress

While we all seek to do this work rapidly and fully, part of the demands of the margins is the recognition that progress can be, at times, incremental. While I now refute the notion that equity must take a lifetime, I acknowledge that on both individual and systemic levels, progress is often micro as opposed to macro.

I believe the margins call on each of us to think about how we can engage in micro-progress. Indeed, part of moving beyond good will is recognizing that good will and harmful micro-aggressions often peacefully coexist. Microaggressions are those statements and questions that may seem innocuous on their own. However, the cumulative impact is quite detrimental. Some research has categorized microaggressions: Microassaults are intentional actions or words to exclude a marginalized group. Microinsults, which emerge from unconscious bias, serve to question or undermine the ability and strength of the object of those insults. Microinvalidations occur when someone's lived experience is questioned or othered or their perception of their lived experience is presumed inaccurate.[5] On many days, you can experience a combination of all of these microaggressions.

Marginalized people encounter microaggressions no matter where they are located in the world and no matter how much power and authority they hold. For example, the microaggressions I confront in the world tend to be:

- So, how'd you get your job?
- Do you have a PhD?
- Where's the president?
- What do Black women think about this issue?
- There's no such thing as microaggressions.
- That wasn't because of your race.
- That wasn't because of your sex.

Many people have faced their own microaggressions. When others deny that experience, not only are they attempting to tell someone what their experience in the world is or should be, they are denying that person's voice and right to share their experience. It reduces their humanity and privileges the humanity of the one who says it didn't happen. Microaggressions are harmful because the daily exposure, the cumulative years of daily microinsults, make life difficult. It is the daily reminder that you're "different" and historically perceived as less than. It's the fact that you're most accepted when people say they don't see color;

however, that means that you're most accepted when people deny a significant part of who you are and what your experience has been.

So, what action must we take as leaders from the margins? Because words can lift up as much as they can destroy, what if we counter microaggressions with microaffirmations? Micro-affirmations are the intentional effort to affirm and lift up an-other. It can be as small as acknowledging the existence or humanity of a fellow human being by finding something kind to say about a peer; witnessing their pain by simply saying, "I believe you"; or witnessing their humanity by saying, "That must have hurt when you experienced that" and not trying to console by diminishing their experience or their hurt. These are small steps that move beyond good will because you are intentionally asking more and demanding more of yourself. The mere acknowl-edgment that microaggressions exist and have an impact moves you into a deeper level of understanding, especially if it is some-thing that has never happened to you.

Choosing When and How to Respond

Earlier in the chapter, I indicated that being a martyr is not the demand of the margins. Rather, one must find the balance be-tween courageously leading and preserving oneself. For exam-ple, as noted earlier, college and university presidents are called upon to make statements about contemporary issues. This is an essential part of using the leadership platform. And, generally, it comes from a hopeful place when people ask for such a statement of protest. However, as Martin Luther King, Jr. once expressed, these symbolic protests, the simple statements of a president, are not as effectual as needed to make change. And, sometimes, they take attention from more effective responses. He wrote:

> If I sought to answer all of the criticisms that cross my desk, my secretaries would be engaged in little else in the course of the day, and I would have no time for constructive work. But since I feel that you are men of genuine good will and your criticisms are sincerely set forth, I would like to answer your statement in what I hope will be patient and reasonable terms.[6]

Further, the responses and statements that are shared often offer only a broad understanding of difficult issues that people of color wrestle daily. They are statements of shallow good will. For some, issues of racism, sexism, classism, homophobia, violence against women, and more are moral and academic issues. They are issues with which they wrestle when a major issue erupts but not as a daily lived experience. For others—those of us on the margins—these are issues that frame portions of or the entirety of our existence. They are emotional and raw. And it may take time to respond because I, too, am a human grieving a lack of justice. Provide yourself the grace and the space to honor your needs as well as those you seek to serve.

Hope in the Margins

In moments of challenge and crises, I do find that I tend more towards hope than outrage. While an effective response likely requires both, it is helpful to know one's natural inclinations. It is important to interrogate those inclinations and understand their origins. Amid the COVID-19 pandemic, I began thinking about hope. Why was that my shelter within the margins? As I delved deeper into my own interior reflections, I began to think about the Middle Passage a great deal, not because it's my area of study or research (in fact, I don't know very much about it from a research perspective) but because that is my origin story.

The Middle Passage, the part of the slave trade journey that brought millions of Africans to be enslaved on US soil in trade for other goods, is known for its inhumane conditions. These conditions included insufficient space to dwell, poor food, rampant disease, and the destruction of one's humanity. This journey—my origin story as an American—has become prominent in my thinking.

In fact, as I stand and look out at the Atlantic from the shores of North Carolina, I have begun to feel a visceral tug toward someone—not something—on the other side of this ocean. The nearly magnetic pull I feel is towards a person who began that harrowing journey and who was one of my foremothers. I gaze out at the ocean and wonder how she felt. What was the experience in her body? She had been captured and, perhaps, sold at least once. I imagine the fear was overwhelming. I look at these waves on a cold December morning, and I try to imagine what her experience was on that boat. She probably couldn't move. She was likely sexually violated. Undoubtedly, the stench of death surrounded her. The motion of the waves and lack of food must have been unbearable at times.

That fateful journey brought her to these shores. I wonder, when the ship stopped, was there any sense of relief or release? She did not know what horrors would await her, horrors that continue to have an impact on our society and her descendants 400 years later. I feel a tug to a spirit on the other side of this ocean. Did she feel all hope was lost? Did it feel like a beginning? For me, that was my beginning. A beginning that, today, feels dangerous to remember.

Johann Baptist Metz, the prominent Catholic theologian, wrote extensively about dangerous memory. For Metz, a political and liberation theologian, our collective memory too often leaves out those who have been marginalized. Metz proposed that foregrounding the memories of those whom history would rather forget—the dispossessed, the victimized, the marginalized—would be dangerous to the status quo by forcing us to look at the political systems that allowed such cruelty to unfold. Metz proclaimed that these dangerous memories are essential in understanding systems, promoting liberation, and, fundamentally, understanding the power and meaning of Christ's suffering on the cross.

For me, those dangerous memories began on the shores of Africa in the body of one woman and were transported to this waterfront in the United States. Are her dangerous memories of fear, terror, hurt, and longing for the ship to stop now mine to proclaim? How do I give voice to her anticipation and subsequent disappointment when she realized what awaited on these shores? Who tells her story and surfaces this dangerous memory that impacts me (and others) even today? As my esteemed colleague Ángel Díaz Miranda shared with me in an email correspondence, "Memory is a fragile thing. More so for those who are immersed in privilege. Memory for them is a device of happiness or resentment, not one of mourning, trauma, or resistance." For those of us who emerge from the margins, our memories are filled with mourning and resistance and are, at times, dangerous.

I believe this longing as I stare at the sea is a dangerous memory whispering in my spirit. Furthermore, I believe that I cannot understand my present without understanding her past. Yuval Noah Harari writes in *Homo Deus,* his 2017 book on human evolution, "Your feelings are the voice of millions of ancestors each of whom managed to survive and reproduce in an unforgiving environment."[7]

Is Harari right that our DNA evolved, and by holding and capturing those memories, hope can be born in such deep despair? Is my hope, my joy, the very nature of my being, inextricably linked to the suffering of those who faced this ocean? And what does that mean for my mission, my calling, my vocation, my work, and my way of being in the world? Does it mean that I am destined to suffer, or does it mean that I have an obligation to remember and to surface and use my voice to articulate the dangerous memory? Does it mean that I must use my voice, a voice epigenetically rooted in her suffering, to give hope to the world around me?

Her experience is now my dangerous memory. It's now in my DNA. A memory of suffering. A memory of doubt. A memory of questioning. And yet, somewhere in that memory, from those shores of Africa, across this rolling ocean, and onto these hateful shores, there is also a memory of courage. A memory of survival. A memory of hope. A memory of perseverance. That's my dangerous memory too. I get up each day to honor that dangerous memory, to emphasize the hope, and to let her know that I pray her trip to these shores has resulted in something good.

For many generations, the hope of that better life relied on death, sweeping through the pearly gates for relief. The sweet freedom found in death is not my only source of hope today. My hope is that we can make this world, this hostile environment, better. My resilience is that if I just take one more step, I, *we*, can change the world. Was that ambition born in the hollows of the ship filled with despair? How could something so beautiful, a natural inclination toward hopeful action, be born under such devastating circumstances? And yet, I have no other way to explain it.

Questions for Reflection

This is demanding work. But leadership is my vocation. I suspect that the margins—with all its joys and demands—are beckoning you as well. As you consider your own path to leadership from the margins, I offer these questions for reflection:

- What is your mission?
- Who do you want to be?
- What are your callings from the margins and the center?
- What dangerous memories do you seek to honor?
- Where and who do you want to lead?

Conclusion
What If?

Mara Falkner, a Sister of the Order of Saint Benedict, poet, and professor emerita of English, once wrote about two little words: *what if*. She wrote:

> The "What if" question gives birth to every work of art, story, scientific discovery, and maybe creation itself. It makes us partners with our daring, hopeful God, who must have asked at the moment of creation, "What if I made a world brimming with possibility, and humans who are free to explore, to wonder, to choose, to love, and to question?"

As we come to the end of this book and our journey together, I invite you to ponder *what if* as you contemplate your next leadership action.

What if, instead of framing your story around what you have accomplished *despite* where you come from, you framed your successes around *because of* where you come from?

What if the margins beckon to you instead of constraining you?

What if, instead of shrinking who you are to fit into the world, you expand the world by sharing your full self and truth?

What if you risk failure and try something completely new? What if stepping outside of your comfort zone means stepping into a brand-new arena of success and opportunity? What if you choose to interpret adversity, pain, and challenges as learning opportunities?

What if you act to support, encourage, and build up others at every opportunity? What if you recognize that the success of others enhances you? What if you intentionally choose to lift up another? What if the other person returns the favor?

What if you stop explaining and start listening to yourself? What if you listened to your spirit and then shared your story? How could it empower others?

What if we act as God's partner and choose to explore, wonder, love, and question together as leaders? What if we have the capacity to not only be transformed by leadership but to transform higher education with our presence, our hope, and our efforts to illuminate a brighter future?

What if you choose to lead from the margins? When you find yourself in the center, what if you turn to others and invite them in? What if you create a community where there is no "center" or "marginal" space, but only radical love, belonging, and hope?

What if you choose hope? There's so much in this world today that is wrong: racism, hatred, and injustice are words you hear and actions you witness all too often. You are called to respond to all of this negativity to help make the world a much better place. Corita Kent wrote, "It is a huge danger to pretend that awful things do not happen. But you need enough hope to keep

going. I am trying to make hope. Flowers grow out of darkness."
What if you choose to make flowers grow out of darkness?

I ask myself *what if* each and every day. The possibilities are invigorating and energizing. I invite you to ask the question along with me and to join me in pursuit of the answer.

NOTES

Introduction

1. Hinton, "Leading from the Margins."
2. Google's English dictionary, provided by Oxford Language, accessed June 21, 2019.
3. Murphy, "Picture a Leader."
4. McGregor, "How Most Leadership Training Programs Fail Women."
5. Paige, "Why Are There So Few Black Women Leaders on College Campuses?"
6. Hinchliffe, "The Female CEOs."
7. Hinchliffe, "The Female CEOs."
8. Soria, Hussein, and Vue, "Leadership for Whom?"

Chapter 1. An Origin Story

1. Opportunity Insights, "Frequently Asked Questions."
2. Opportunity Insights, "Frequently Asked Questions."
3. According to the US Department of Education (https://www2 .ed.gov/policy/gen/guid/fpco/ferpa/index.html), the Family Educational Rights and Privacy Act (FERPA) (20 U.S.C. § 1232g; 34 CFR Part 99) is a federal law that protects the privacy of student education records. The law applies to all schools that receive funds under an applicable program of the US Department of Education.

Chapter 2. Finding My Life's Work

1. Benedictine Institute, "Dignity of Work."
2. Jaschik, "Obama vs. Art History."

Chapter 3. Leading While Black

1. Jackson and Harris, "African American Female College and University Presidents," 132.
2. Jackson and Harris, "African American Female College and University Presidents," 131.
3. Korn Ferry, "The Black P&L Leader."
4. Roberts et al., "Beating the Odds."
5. McCallum, "Giving Back."
6. McCallum, "Giving Back," 147.
7. Jackson and Harris, "African American Female College and University Presidents."
8. McDonald, Keeves, and Westphal, "One Step Forward."

Chapter 4. Leading While Female

1. De Bray et al., *Digest of Education Statistics 2019*, ch. 3, and Johnson, *Pipelines, Pathways, and Institutional Leadership*.
2. Kelly, "Though More Women."
3. McChesney, *Representation and Pay of Women of Color*.
4. Kramer, "Recognizing Workplace Challenges."
5. Waring, "African-American Female College Presidents."
6. See, for example, Eagly and Johannesen-Schmidt, "The Leadership Styles of Women and Men."
7. Kezar and Lester, "Breaking the Barriers of Essentialism."
8. Sandberg with Scovell, *Lean In*.
9. Brzezinski, *Knowing Your Value*.
10. Kramer and Harris, "The Goldilocks Dilemma."
11. Rosette et al., "Race Matters for Women Leaders."
12. Correll et al., "Inside the Black Box."
13. Ryan and Haslam, "The Glass Cliff."
14. Korn Ferry, "The Black P&L Leader."
15. Waring, "African-American Female College Presidents," 34.
16. Forsythe, "Effect of Applicant's Clothing."
17. Modestino, "Coronavirus Child-Care Crisis."

Chapter 5. Navigating toward Leadership from the Rural South

1. Lumby, "Disappearing Gender," 29.
2. Lumby, "Disappearing Gender," 37.
3. Kelly and Lobao, "The Social Bases."
4. Cramer, *Politics of Resentment*, 12.
5. Cramer, *Politics of Resentment*, 89.
6. Enke and Zenk, "Farmwomen in the Academy," 653.
7. Malcolm X, "The Black Revolution."
8. Edsall and Edsall, *Chain Reaction*.
9. Cerullo, "High School Senior's Funny Yearbook Quote."
10. United States Department of Agriculture Economic Research Service, "Rural Poverty and Well-Being."
11. Dudley-Marling and Dudley-Marling, "Inclusive Leadership and Poverty," 40.

Chapter 6. Leadership Theory from the Margins

1. Aspen Institute, "Renewal and Progress."
2. National Center for Education Statistics, "Digest of Education Statistics 2016, table 302.10."
3. Bransberger, Falkenstern, and Lane, *Knocking at the College Door*.
4. American Council on Education, "American College President Study."
5. We the Protesters, "Campus Demands."
6. Evje, "Quick: Define Leadership."
7. Frei and Morriss, "Begin with Trust."
8. McGregor, "Even among Harvard MBAs."
9. Jones and Shorter-Gooden, *Shifting*, 6–7.
10. George, "The Truth about Authentic Leaders."
11. "Before I Can Tell," Quote Catalog.
12. Collins, "Level 5 Leadership."
13. Rumi, "Say Yes Quickly."
14. "Quotation #4633," Quotations Page.

Chapter 7. The Vocational Cycle to Support Institutional Justice

1. McCallum, "Giving Back" and Waring, "African-American Female College Presidents."
2. Hayes, *Hagar's Daughters*, 5.
3. Patitu and Hinton, "The Experiences of African American Women," 79–93.

4. Jones and Shorter-Gooden, *Shifting*, 7.
5. Evans and Herr, "The Influence of Racism and Sexism," 132.
6. Moore, "Stories of Vocation," 218–239.
7. Moore, "Stories of Vocation," 218–239, and Patitu and Hinton, "The Experiences of African American Women."
8. Palmer, "A Life Lived Whole," para 3.
9. Palmer, "A Life Lived Whole," para 2.
10. Jinkins, "The Professor's Vocations," 64.
11. Gonzales, "Why Black Workers" and Kochhar, Parker, and Igielnik, "Majority of U.S. Workers."
12. Weller, "African Americans Face."
13. Hinton, "In Need of a Newer Model," 43.

Chapter 8. Senior Leadership in Higher Education

1. Cole and Harper, "Race and Rhetoric."

Chapter 9. On Courage and Gratitude

1. Roberts et al., "Beating the Odds."
2. D'Angelo, "How to Find a Mentor."
3. Roberts et al., "Beating the Odds."
4. Korn Ferry, "The Black P&L Leader."
5. Holmes, "Introduction: An Overview of African American College Presidents."
6. Waring, "African-American Female College Presidents," 37.
7. Jackson and Harris, "African American Female College and University Presidents," 132.

Chapter 10. Interrogating the Demands of the Margins

1. Hinton, "The Whisper of Dangerous Memory."
2. Boyatzis, Richard E., and Annie McKee. *Resonant Leadership: Renewing Yourself and Connecting with Others Through Mindfulness, Hope, and Compassion.* Boston, MA: Harvard Business School Press, 2005.
3. Manne, *Down Girl*, 22.
4. King, "Letter from a Birmingham City Jail."
5. Sue et al., "Racial Microaggressions in Everyday Life."
6. King, "Letter from a Birmingham City Jail."
7. Harari, *Homo Deus*, 397.

BIBLIOGRAPHY

American Council on Education. "American College President Study." Last accessed August 4, 2022. https://www.acenet.edu/news-room/Pages /American-College-President-Study.aspx.

Aspen Institute Task Force on the Future of the College Presidency. "Renewal and Progress: Strengthening Higher Education Leadership in a Time of Rapid Change." Washington, DC: Aspen Institute, 2017. https://www.aspeninstitute.org/publications/renewal-progress -strengthening-higher-education-leadership-time-rapid-change.

"Before I Can Tell My Life What I Want to Do with It, I Must Listen to My Life Telling Me Who I Am," Quote Catalog, accessed June 8, 2023, https://quotecatalog.com/quote/parker-j-palmer-before-i-can-te -9aJGwZ1.

Benedictine Institute at Saint John's University. "Dignity of Work." *Benedictine Bits*, no date. https://www.csbsju.edu/images /Benedictine%20Institute/Benedictine%20Bits%20Dignity%20 of%20Work.pdf.

Bransberger, Peace, Colleen Falkenstern, and Patrick Lane. *Knocking at the College Door: Projections of High School Graduates* (Boulder, CO: Western Interstate Commission for Higher Education, 2020), https://www.wiche.edu/wp-content/uploads/2020/12/Knocking -pdf-for-website.pdf.

Brzezinski, Mika. *Knowing Your Value: Women, Money, and Getting What You're Worth* (New York: Hachette Books, 2012).

Cerullo, Megan. "High School Senior's Funny Yearbook Quote about 'Sounding White' Goes Viral." *New York Daily News*, May 4, 2017.

https://www.nydailynews.com/news/national/high-school-senior
-yearbook-quote-viral-article-1.3138021.

Cole, Eddie R., and Shaun R. Harper. "Race and Rhetoric: An Analysis of College Presidents' Statements on Campus Racial Incidents." *Journal of Diversity in Higher Education* 10, no. 4 (2017): 318–33.

Collins, Jim. "Level 5 Leadership: The Triumph of Humility and Fierce Resolve." *Harvard Business Review*, January 1, 2001. https://hbr.org /2001/01/level-5-leadership-the-triumph-of-humility-and-fierce -resolve-2.

Correll, Shelley J., Katherine R. Weisshaar, Allison T. Wynn, and JoAnne Delfino Wehner. "Inside the Black Box of Organizational Life: The Gendered Language of Performance Assessment." *American Sociological Review* 85, no. 6 (December 2020): 1022–50. doi:10.1177/0003122420962080.

Cramer, Katherine. *The Politics of Resentment: Rural Consciousness in Wisconsin and the Rise of Scott Walker* (Chicago: University of Chicago Press, 2016.)

D'Angelo, Matt. "How to Find a Mentor." *Business News Daily*, July 7, 2022. https://www.businessnewsdaily.com/6248-how-to-find -mentor.html.

De Brey, Cristobal., Thomas D. Snyder, Anlan Zhang, and Sally A. Dillow. "Chapter 3: Postsecondary Education" in *Digest of Education Statistics 2019* (NCES 2021-009) Washington, DC: National Center for Education Statistics, Institute of Education Sciences, US Department of Education, 2021. https://nces.ed.gov/pubs2021 /2021009.pdf

Dudley-Marling, Curt, and Anne Dudley-Marling. "Inclusive Leadership and Poverty," in *Leadership for Increasingly Diverse Schools*, ed. George Theoharis and Martin Scanlan (New York: Routledge, 2015), 39–57.

Eagly, Alice H., and Mary C. Johannesen-Schmidt. "The Leadership Styles of Women and Men," *Journal of Social Issues* 57 (2001): 781–97.

Edsall, Mary D., and Thomas Byrne Edsall. *Chain Reaction: The Impact of Race, Rights, and Taxes on American Politics* (New York: W. W. Norton, 1992).

Enke, Kathryn A. E., and Leslie R. Zenk. "Farmwomen in the Academy: Rurality and Leadership in Higher Education." *International Journal of Leadership in Education* 24, no. 5 (2021): 653–69. doi:10.1080/136 03124.2019.1690703.

Evans, Kathy M., and Edwin L. Herr. "The Influence of Racism and Sexism in the Career Development of African American Women." *Journal of Multicultural Counseling & Development* 19, no. 3 (July 1991): 130–135.

Evje, "Quick: Define Leadership." *Inc.*, January 30, 2013, https://www.inc.com/brian-evje/quick-define-leadership.html.

Forsythe, Sandra M. "Effect of Applicant's Clothing on Interviewer's Decision to Hire." *Journal of Applied Social Psychology* 20 (1990): 1579–95. doi:10.1111/j.1559-1816.1990.tb01494.x.

Frei, Frances X., and Anne Morriss. "Begin with Trust." *Harvard Business Review*, May–June 2020. https://hbr.org/2020/05/begin-with-trust.

George, Bill. "The Truth about Authentic Leaders." *Forbes*, July 6, 2016. https://www.forbes.com/sites/hbsworkingknowledge/2016/07/06/the-truth-about-authentic-leaders.

Gonzales, Matt. "Why Black Workers Are Seeking New Opportunities." Society for Human Resource Management, Alexandria, VA. Last modified February 22, 2022. https://www.shrm.org/resourcesandtools/hr-topics/behavioral-competencies/global-and-cultural-effectiveness/pages/why-black-workers-are-seeking-new-opportunities.aspx.

Harari, Yuval Noah. *Homo Deus: A Brief History for Tomorrow* (New York: HarperCollins, 2017).

Hayes, Diana. *Hagar's Daughters: Womanist Ways of Being in the World* (Notre Dame, IN: Saint Mary's College, 1995).

Hinchliffe, Emma. "The Female CEOs on This Year's Fortune 500 Just Broke Three All-Time Records." *Fortune*, June 2, 2021. https://fortune.com/2021/06/02/female-ceos-fortune-500-2021-women-ceo-list-roz-brewer-walgreens-karen-lynch-cvs-thasunda-brown-duckett-tiaa.

Hinton, Mary. "In Need of a Newer Model." *Diverse Issues in Higher Education* 27 (2010): 43.

Hinton, Mary. "Leading from the Margins." Filmed October 2019 at TEDxStCloud, St. Cloud, MN. Video. https://www.ted.com/talks/mary_dana_hinton_leading_from_the_margins.

Hinton, Mary. "The Whisper of Dangerous Memory." Interfaith America. Last modified May 17, 2022. https://www.interfaithamerica.org/the-whisper-of-dangerous-memory.

Holmes, Sharon L. "Introduction: An Overview of African American College Presidents: A Game of Two Steps Forward, One Step

Backward, and Standing Still." *Journal of Negro Education* 73, no. 1 (winter 2004).

Jackson, Sandra, and Sandra Harris. "African American Female College and University Presidents: Experiences and Perceptions of Barriers to the Presidency." *Journal of Women in Educational Leadership* 5, no. 2 (April 2007): 119–37. http://digitalcommons.unl.edu/jwel/7.

Jaschik, Scott. "Obama vs. Art History." Inside Higher Ed. Last modified January 31, 2014. https://www.insidehighered.com/news/2014/01 /31/obama-becomes-latest-politician-criticize-liberal-arts-discipline.

Jinkins, Michael. "The Professor's Vocations: Reflections on the Teacher as Writer." *Teaching Theology & Religion* 7, no. 2 (April 2004): 64–70.

Johnson, Heather L. *Pipelines, Pathways, and Institutional Leadership: An Update on the Status of Women in Higher Education* (Washington, DC: American Council on Higher Education, 2017).

Jones, Charisse, and Kumea Shorter-Gooden. *Shifting: The Double Lives of Black Women in America* (New York: Harper Perennial, 2004).

Kelly, Bridget Turner. "Though More Women Are on College Campuses, Climbing the Professor Ladder Remains a Challenge." Brookings Institution, Washington, DC. Last modified March 29, 2019. https://www.brookings.edu/blog/brown-center-chalkboard/2019 /03/29/though-more-women-are-on-college-campuses-climbing-the -professor-ladder-remains-a-challenge.

Kelly, Paige, and Linda Lobao. "The Social Bases of Rural-Urban Political Divides: Social Status, Work, and Sociocultural Beliefs." *Rural Sociology* 84, no. 4 (2019): 669–705. doi:10.1111/ruso.12256.

Kezar, Adrianna, and Jamie Lester. "Breaking the Barriers of Essential-ism in Leadership Research: Positionality as a Promising Approach." *Feminist Formations* 22, no. 1 (2010): 163–85.

King, Jr., Martin Luther. "Letter from a Birmingham City Jail." American Friends Service Committee, Philadelphia, May 1968.

Kochhar, Rakesh, Kim Parker, and Ruth Igielnik. "Majority of U.S. Workers Changing Jobs Are Seeing Real Wage Gains." Pew Research Center, Washington, DC. Last modified July 28, 2022. https://www .pewresearch.org/social-trends/2022/07/28/majority-of-u-s -workers-changing-jobs-are-seeing-real-wage-gains.

Korn Ferry. "The Black P&L Leader: Insights and Lessons from Senior Black P&L Leaders in Corporate America," 2019. Last accessed July 26, 2022. https://infokf.kornferry.com/The-Black-PandL

-Leader-Report.html?utm_source=website&utm_medium
=pressrelease&utm_term=black-p&l-SEO-article&utm_content
=whitepaper&utm_campaign=21-06-dei&_ga=2.155284978
.891816712.1686344622-1214503885.1686344620.

Kramer, Andie. "Recognizing Workplace Challenges Faced by Black
Women Leaders," *Forbes,* January 7, 2020. https://www.forbes.com
/sites/andiekramer/2020/01/07/recognizing-workplace-challenges
-faced-by-black-women-leaders.

Kramer, Andrea S., and Alton B. Harris. "The Goldilocks Dilemma: Why
Career Advancement Is So Much Harder for Women than Men and
What Women Can Do to Change That." *Porchlight Blog,* May 4, 2016.
https://www.porchlightbooks.com/blog/changethis/2016/the
-goldilocks-dilemma-why-career-advancement-is-so-much-harder
-for-women-than-men-and-what-women-can-do-to-change-that.

Lumby, Jacky. "Disappearing Gender: Choices in Identity," in *Women
Leading Education across the Continents: Sharing the Spirit, Fanning the
Flame*, ed. Helen C. Sobehart (Lanham, MD: Rowman & Littlefield
Education, 2009), 29–38.

Malcolm X. *See* X, Malcolm

Manne, Kate. *Down Girl.* (New York: Oxford University Press, 2018).

McCallum, Carmen. "Giving Back to the Community: How African
Americans Envision Utilizing Their PhD." *Journal of Negro Education*
86, no. 2 (2017): 138–53. doi:10.7709/jnegroeducation.86.2.0138.

McChesney, Jasper. *Representation and Pay of Women of Color in the Higher
Education Workforce.* (Knoxville, TN: CUPA-HR, 2018). https://www
.cupahr.org/wp-content/uploads/CUPA-HR-Brief-Women-Of-Color
-1.pdf.

McDonald, Michael L., Gareth D. Keeves, and James D. Westphal.
"One Step Forward, One Step Back: White Male Top Manager
Organizational Identification and Helping Behavior toward Other
Executives Following the Appointment of a Female or Racial
Minority CEO." University of Michigan. Last modified February 15,
2018. http://ns.umich.edu/Releases/2018/Feb18/One-step-forward
-two-steps-back-study-20180213.pdf.

McGregor, Jena. "Even among Harvard MBAs, Few Black Women Ever
Reach Corporate America's Top Rungs." *Washington Post,* February 20, 2018. https://www.washingtonpost.com/news/on-leadership
/wp/2018/02/20/even-among-harvard-mbas-few-black-women-ever
-reach-corporate-americas-top-rungs.

McGregor, Jena. "How Most Leadership Training Programs Fail Women." *Washington Post,* October 23, 2017. www.washingtonpost.com/news /on-leadership/wp/2017/10/23/how-most-leadership-training -programs-fail-women.

Modestino, Alicia Sasser. "Coronavirus Child-Care Crisis Will Set Women Back a Generation." *Washington Post,* July 29, 2020. https://www .washingtonpost.com/us-policy/2020/07/29/childcare-remote -learning-women-employment.

Moore, Mary Elizabeth Mullino. "Stories of Vocation: Education for Vocational Discernment." *Religious Education* 103, no. 2 (April 2008): 218–239.

Murphy, Heather. "Picture a Leader. Is She a Woman?" *New York Times,* March 16, 2018. www.nytimes.com/2018/03/16/health/women -leadership-workplace.html.

National Center for Education Statistics, Institute of Education Sciences, US Department of Education. "Digest of Education Statistics 2016, table 302.10: Recent High School Completers and Their Enrollment in 2-year and 4-year Colleges, by Sex: 1960 through 2015." Last accessed August 4, 2022. https://nces.ed.gov/programs/digest/d16 /tables/dt16_302.10.asp.

Opportunity Insights. "Frequently Asked Questions." Last accessed May 29, 2023. https://opportunityinsights.org/policy/frequently -asked-questions.

Paige, DeAsia. "Why Are There So Few Black Women Leaders on College Campuses?" *The Nation,* October 1, 2018. www.thenation.com/article /why-are-there-so-few-black-women-leaders-on-college-campuses.

Palmer, Parker J. "A Life Lived Whole." *Yes Magazine,* November 9, 2004. http://www.yesmagazine.org/issues/healing-resistance/a-life-lived -whole.

Patitu, Carl Logan, and Kandace G. Hinton. "The Experiences of African American Women Faculty and Administrators in Higher Education: Has Anything Changed?" *New Directions for Student Services* no. 104 (winter 2003): 79–93.

"Quotation #4633," Quotation Page, http://www.quotationspage.com /quote/4633.html.

Roberts, Laura Morgan, Anthony J. Mayo, Robin J. Ely, and David A. Thomas. "Beating the Odds." *Harvard Business Review,* March– April 2018. https://hbr.org/2018/03/beating-the-odds.

Rosette, Ashleigh Shelby, Christy Zhou Koval, Anvi Ma, and Robert Livingston, "Race Matters for Women Leaders: Intersectional Effects on Agentic Deficiencies and Penalties." *Leadership Quarterly* 27, no. 3 (2016): 429–45. doi:10.1016/j.leaqua.2016.01.008.

Rumi, "Say Yes Quickly," Threshold Society, https://sufism.org/origins /rumi/rumi-excerpts/poems-of-rumi-tr-by-coleman-barks-published -by-threshold-books-2.

Ryan, Michelle K., and S. Alexander Haslam. "The Glass Cliff: Evidence That Women Are Over-Represented in Precarious Leadership Positions." *British Journal of Management* 16 (2005): 81–90. doi:10.1111/j.1467-8551.2005.00433.x.

Sandberg, Sheryl, with Nell Scovell, *Lean In: Women, Work and the Will to Lead*. (New York: Alfred A. Knopf, 2013).

Smith, Anna Deavere. *Talk to Me: Listening Between the Lines*. (New York: Random House, 2000).

Soria, Krista M., Deeqa Hussein, and Carolyn Vue. "Leadership for Whom? Socioeconomic Factors Predicting Undergraduate Students' Positional Leadership Participation." *Journal of Leadership Education* 13, no. 1 (2014): 14–30. doi:10.12806/V13/I1/R2.

Sue, Derald Wing, Christina M. Capodilupo, Gina C. Torino, Jennifer M. Bucceri, Aisha M. B. Holder, Kevin L. Nadal, and Marta Esquilin. "Racial Microaggressions in Everyday Life: Implications for Clinical Practice." *American Psychologist* 62, no. 4 (May–June 2007): 271–286. doi:10.1037/0003-066x.62.4.271.

United States Department of Agriculture Economic Research Service. "Rural Poverty and Well-Being." Last accessed August 9, 2022. https://www.ers .usda.gov/topics/rural-economy-population/rural-poverty-well-being.

Waring, Anna L. "African-American Female College Presidents: Self Conceptions of Leadership." *Journal of Leadership & Organizational Studies* 9, no. 3 (2003), 31–44. doi:10.1177/107179190300900305.

Weller, Christian E. "African Americans Face Systematic Obstacles to Getting Good Jobs." Center for American Progress, Washington, DC, December 5, 2019. https://www.americanprogress.org/article /african-americans-face-systematic-obstacles-getting-good-jobs.

We the Protesters. "Campus Demands." Last accessed August 4, 2022. https://www.thedemands.org.

X, Malcolm. "The Black Revolution: April 8, 1964, New York City," in *Malcolm X Speaks: Selected Speeches and Statements*, ed. George Breitman (New York: Grove Press, 1965) 45–57.

INDEX

Harari, Yuval Noah, 176–77
harassment, 49–50
Harper, Shaun R., 137
Harris, Sandra, 159
Haslam, S. Alexander, 71
Hayes, Diana, 115–16
Heatherington, Laurie, 156–57
helpfulness, 70–71
Herr, Edwin L., 118
higher education: access to, 52–54; and demographic changes in students, 41, 53–54, 92–93, 127; need for change in, 52–54, 127; as urban, 80–81
higher education leadership: challenges facing, 62–63, 91–92, 145; defiance as leading author to, 31–32; and desire mindset, 144–46; dialectics in, 115–19; goals of, 92; interest in by first-generation and low-income students, 8; as about leader, 134–37; and listening tours, 139; and need for change, 52–54, 127; as not about leader, 138–40; percentage of women in, 7, 66, 93; percentage of women of color in, 7, 67; scrutiny of, 135–36, 137; and sponsorship and mentorship, 154–60; statements and responses by, 173–74; and stewardship, 134. *See also* institutional change; presidents, college and university
Hinton, Judy, 41–42
Hinton, Kandace G., 117, 120
Hinton, Susie: and dignity of work, 34–35; education of, 37; and education of author, 26–28, 30–31, 37; and grit and resilience, 30–31; marginalization of, 35–38; and titles, 23
Hollins Opportunity for Promise through Education (HOPE), 105–6
Hollins University: HOPE scholarship, 105–6; inauguration address, 59; as return to South for author, 83–84; and vocational alignment of author, 141
Holmes, Sharon L., 155–56
hope, 174–78, 180–81
humanity: and disagreements, 134–35; and microaffirmations, 173; and microaggressions, 172; mother's ability to share, 26
humility, 103–4

identity: and acknowledging personal experiences, 16–17; as defined in relationship to the center, 2, 24, 81–84; and geography, 79, 80; reflection on, 110; and representation, 16–17; as term, 79; of women as broad/multifaceted, 79. *See also* authenticity
imposter syndrome, 107, 161
income, in Opportunity Atlas, 19. *See also* socioeconomic status; students, low-income
institutional change: and alignment with vocation and occupational choices, 124, 126, 128, 140–42; and courage, 64; and desire mindset, 144–46; and institutional climate, 114–15, 123–24; and institutional life and governance, 113, 122–23; pressure on leaders from margins for, 111–12; reflection on, 129; resistance to, 124; and serving vs. transforming, 121; and Vocational Cycle to Support Institutional Justice, 113, 119–29; and vulnerability, 124
institutional climate, 114–15, 123–24
institutional life and governance, 113, 122–23
institutional mission, 123
intentionality, 106–7
intersectionality: of author, 25, 64; of poverty, 84; and women of color, 66–69

mission, institutional, 123
mission-driven leadership, 99–106, 165, 166, 177–78
Moore, Mary Elizabeth Mullino, 120
mothering, 122, 123
Mount Saint Mary College, 158–59
Murphy Brown, 157

Obama, Barack, 42
occupational choices: and alignment with institution, 140–42; and authenticity, 121–22, 123; and career vs. family dynamic, 76, 157; and first-generation students, 8, 42–43; and institutional climate, 124; interest in higher education leadership by first-generation and low-income students, 8; race and leaving jobs, 126; and socioeconomic status, 8, 42–43; and Vocational Cycle to Support Institutional Justice, 113, 121–22, 123, 124, 128. *See also* work
opportunity: and geography, 18–19; and glass cliff, 71–72, 77–78; and humility, 103–4; and mission/vocation, 102–4; and poverty, 84; reflection on, 110, 180; what-ifs, 180
Opportunity Atlas, 18–19
origin stories: of author, 18–33; and defiance, 20–28; of reader, 32–33
outperform, need to, 56–60, 116–17
overwork vs. underutilization dialectic, 115, 116–17

Palmer, Parker, 100, 121, 123
parenting, single, 19
Patitu, Carl Logan, 117, 120
personal context. *See* context, personal
Pinson, Ed, 134
place-based resentment, 80
poverty: of author, 17, 21, 30, 31; and geography, 18–19, 84; and intersectionality, 84; and opportunity,

84; and vulnerability, 84, 85. *See also* socioeconomic status
power vs. powerlessness dialectic, 115–16
present, mission and focus on, 105
presidents, college and university: average tenure of, 91; challenges facing, 62–63, 91–92; demographics of, 93; focus on racial firsts, 55–56; and listening tours, 139; percentage of women, 7, 66, 93; percentage of women of color, 7, 93; vs. presidency, 134; and racial reckoning, 62–63, 173–74; and scrutiny, 135–36, 137; statements and responses, 173–74; and stewardship, 134. *See also* higher education leadership
privilege, acknowledging, 168

quiet, 165–66

race: and defiance, 24–26; and discouragement by community, 82–83; and expectations of failure, 32; and geographic aspects of opportunity, 18–19; and leaving jobs, 126; and marginalization of author, 2–3, 7, 17–19; and power vs. powerlessness dialectic, 115–16. *See also* scholars of color; students of color; women of color and leadership
race and leadership: and community service, 56, 59–60; double bind of leadership by women of color, 67–68; and glass cliff, 72; and marginalization of leaders, 2–3, 5, 7–8; and need to outperform, 56–60, 116–17; and perception by others, 61–63; and pressure for institutional change, 111–12; reflection on, 65; research on, 56–60; and resilience, 56–59; and sponsorship, 154–56, 157–58; as threat to others, 49–50, 62. *See also* women of color and leadership

women of color leaders: and authenticity, 95–96; in author's childhood, 73–74; college presidents, 7, 93; disengagement by, 118; double bind of, 67–68; as doubly marginalized, 2–3, 5, 7–8, 19, 67–68; and intersectionality, 66–69

work: author's early jobs, 41–42; and career vs. family dynamic, 76, 157; dignity of, 34–35; and harassment, 49–50; from home, 77; underutilization vs. overwork dialectic, 115, 116–17; women's qualities in, 120. *See also* occupational choices

writing and vulnerability, 125

X, Malcolm, 82

Zenk, Leslie R., 80–81